A Short History of Wisconsin

Also by Erika Janik
*Odd Wisconsin: Amusing, Perplexing, and
Unlikely Stories from Wisconsin's Past*

A SHORT HISTORY OF
Wisconsin

ERIKA JANIK

WISCONSIN HISTORICAL SOCIETY PRESS

Published by the Wisconsin Historical Society Press
Publishers since 1855

© 2010 by State Historical Society of Wisconsin

Publication of this book was made possible in part by a grant from the Alice E. Smith fellowship fund.

For permission to reuse material from *A Short History of Wisconsin* (ISBN 978-0-87020-440-1), please access www.copyright.com or contact the Copyright Clearance Center, Inc. (CCC), 222 Rosewood Drive, Danvers, MA 01923, 978-750-8400. CCC is a not-for-profit organization that provides licenses and registration for a variety of users.

wisconsin**history**.org

Photographs identified with WHi or WHS are from the Society's collections; address requests to reproduce these photos to the Visual Materials Archivist at the Wisconsin Historical Society, 816 State Street, Madison, WI 53706.

Printed in Wisconsin, U.S.A.
Designed by Percolator Graphic Design

14   13   12   11   10   1   2   3   4   5

Library of Congress Cataloging-in-Publication Data
Janik, Erika.
    A short history of Wisconsin / Erika Janik.
      p. cm.
    Includes bibliographical references and index.
    ISBN 978-0-87020-440-1 (pbk. : alk. paper)
    1. Wisconsin—History. 2. Wisconsin—Social conditions.
    3. Wisconsin—Politics and government. I. Title.
    F581.J36 2010
    977.5—dc22

                                                   2009037497

Front cover images:

Antique photo frame—iStockphoto.com

Postage stamp design from centennial stamp design contest, 1948—WHi Image ID 35733

To Matt, for making Wisconsin,
and my little place in it, feel like home

CONTENTS

INTRODUCTION

WHEN YOU SAY YOU'RE FROM WISCONSIN, you usually get a slight nod of recognition. But mention a particular Wisconsin city, like Menominee or even Madison, and people outside the state may draw a blank.

For people from Wisconsin, however, the state's name brings to mind a singular place with unique qualities. Even if much of our landscape has begun to resemble the rest of the country—parking lots, strip malls, interstate highways, housing subdivisions—there is still something different, even remarkable, about this place. Wisconsinites are unmistakably proud—though in a modest, stereotypically Midwestern way. They don't need to tell you that Wisconsin is better—they just know it, even as they graciously allow other places to boast their superiority.

I first visited and now live in the state. My parents grew up in Illinois and, like all good Illinoisans, often vacationed in Wisconsin in the summer. Even after they moved to a town just outside Seattle, Wisconsin remained their summertime destination. When I was a child, my Wisconsin was rolling hills, fireflies, farms, blaring tornado sirens (though I had no idea what they were), and lightning that cut across the sky in an angry gash. It was the flashy, touristy charms of the Wisconsin Dells, the quiet grace of Taliesin, the bewildering collections of jewelry, dolls, and pipe organs at the House on the Rock, and the truly bizarre Don Q Inn with its theme rooms, barber chairs in the lobby, and rundown passenger plane out front. It was water towers with town names painted on the side—proclaiming themselves to the fields and surrounding towns—and cemeteries located right in town. And it was unlike anything I knew back home in Redmond, Washington.

I came from a place rich in natural beauty—the Cascade Mountains, Puget Sound, the towering evergreen trees. Wisconsin is not generally considered quite as magnificent, but this humbler landscape, whose idiosyncratic charm more than makes up for what it lacks in grandness, grabbed hold and never left me. Perhaps that is why I now call Wisconsin home.

Everything I do now is a product of this place and its past: from the produce and cheese I buy at the farmers market to the roads I travel on my bike to the giant pretzel I order at Mader's German Restaurant in Milwaukee. I am the beneficiary of all the people and traditions and landscapes of Wisconsin. Wisconsin's history is a record of all that has happened here, two hundred years ago and two minutes ago. We can read it not just to find the big events and famous names, but to find ourselves as well. History is what we see no matter where we look.

Natural and human histories are intimately and inseparably intertwined in Wisconsin. Wisconsin's landscape has been used for centuries by different people for different purposes: first for subsistence by Indians, then for fur trading, and then for fishing, shipping, logging, mining, farming, manufacturing, and tourism. Wisconsin could claim to be many things—the land of beer, manufacturing, and water parks—but it has chosen to be "America's Dairyland," calling to mind a pastoral wholesomeness of green grass and grazing Holsteins. Wisconsin also boasts a rich political history, symbolized most strongly by Bob La Follette and the Progressive Party but also by the state's role in the history of the Republican Party and by the "sewer" socialists who ran Milwaukee in the early twentieth century.

While we tend to think of American history as beginning in the east in 1620, particularly in Plymouth, Massachusetts, and moving westward, Wisconsin's story reminds us that our nation's history was shaped not only by what happened in seventeenth-century Massachusetts, but in seventeenth-century Green Bay. Wisconsin's story is unique, but it is also part of a larger American narrative of development and change.

GEOGRAPHY
OF PLACE

ALL HISTORY HAPPENS IN SOME PLACE. The names, facts, and dates in history books sometimes leave the impression that the past exists only on paper and between two covers. But the past is all around us, and Wisconsin is the site of more than one hundred centuries of human history. When we cross a bridge or hike in any of our parks, we share the space once traversed by Jesuit missionaries or French fur traders. On at least one morning during the past fourteen thousand years, Native Americans pursued game just outside your window. Less than a mile from where you're sitting, a pair of surveyors made notes about the landscape one hundred and fifty years ago, as they laid out the boundaries of suburban roads, city blocks, and rural farms.

Human history exerts an effect on place. In turn, the nature of a place, its physical landscape and climate, affects what can or cannot happen there. Wisconsin is bordered on the east by Lake Michigan and on the west by the Mississippi River (mostly). To the north and south it is bounded not by natural features but by human imagination: a line run across the prairies by surveyors in 1832 separates us from Illinois, while another line run in 1847 divides us from Michigan's Upper Peninsula. The eastern lakeshore is generally low and sandy or marshy, with only a few harbors deep enough to handle large ships. The western edge of our state is formed of immense bluffs overlooking the Mississippi, punctuated by steep ravines, or coulees. The southern border runs mostly through nearly flat, fertile land watered by sluggish, shallow rivers. The northern boundary crosses through dark forest, relieved by high wetlands and eventually by the lakes that draw thousands of tourists each summer.

These four principal habitats—eastern lowlands, southern prairies, western valleys, and northern forests—overlap and blend into one another in the interior. From east to west in the southern part of Wisconsin, the rich prairie becomes increasingly hilly, until, west of Madison, few large tracts of perfectly level land can be found. The northern forest is quite dense above a line from Green Bay to Minneapolis. It becomes gradually thinner as one travels southward, until it gives way to open lands along a line roughly from Green Bay to Prairie du Chien. Many unique, smaller landscapes, such as the Door Peninsula and the Kettle Moraine, intersect the four major ones.

Human history happened first in Wisconsin's river valleys, which provided easy transportation, nutritious soil for growing food, and diverse habitats for game animals and birds. The rivers tend to flow either northeast into the Great Lakes or southwest into the Mississippi. In many places one can stand on a ridge between two streams, one headed for the icy waters of the North Atlantic and the other for the sultry swamps around New Orleans. Besides the Mississippi, several other rivers have helped shape Wisconsin history. The state is bisected north to south by the Wisconsin River, which starts in the forest near the Michigan line at Lac Vieux Desert and runs south to Portage, where it veers southwest before emptying into the Mississippi. Other important waterways that flow into the Mississippi are the Black, the Chippewa, and the St. Croix rivers in the northwest, and the Rock River in the south. The most important rivers running in the opposite direction are the Fox, the Wolf, and the Milwaukee, which empty into Lake Michigan.

Today's rivers, lakes, and landforms are largely the result of glaciers drifting slowly down from the north during successive ice ages. Glaciers, some of which were as much as a mile thick, repeatedly bulldozed the state. The last of them was the Laurentian Ice Sheet, whose petallike lobes stretched over northern and eastern

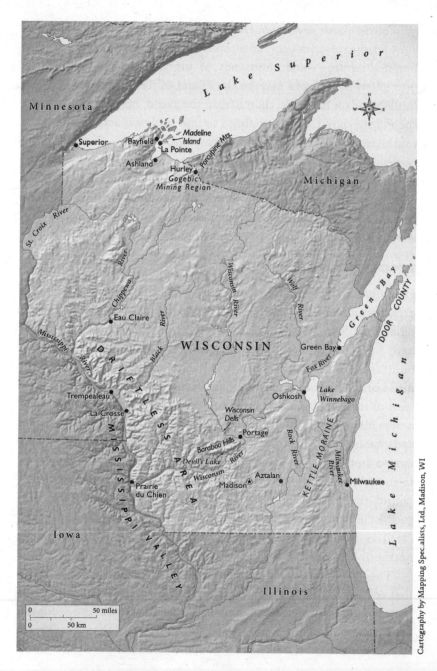

Cartography by Mapping Specialists, Ltd., Madison, WI

Wisconsin about seventeen thousand years ago. In their wake, glaciers left heaps of debris called moraines, thin soil—good for trees but not farming—and thousands of orphan glaciers that melted into lakes. Minnesota may be the "Land of Ten Thousand Lakes," but Wisconsin has more than fifteen thousand, ranging in size from the 137,708-acre Lake Winnebago to one- and two-acre springs. The southwestern third of the state was untouched by these glaciers, however, leaving unique rock formations such as the Wisconsin Dells, Devil's Lake, and the Baraboo Hills. This so-called "driftless area" contains many ancient landscapes that Wisconsin's native peoples have considered uniquely powerful and important.

ANCIENT PEOPLES

People always occupied Wisconsin. The Menominee and Ho-Chunk each preserve ancient narratives that place them here long before written records. In Kenosha and Crawford counties, archaeologists have found the remains of mastodons bearing evidence of human hunting dating from about 12,300 BCE. Members of these communities of First Americans, known as Paleo-Indians, followed the retreat of the glacial ice northward across Wisconsin. They developed a nomadic lifestyle that allowed them to follow the flow of game and changes in the availability of plants and other resources as they moved from place to place. They had to be shrewd and adaptable to survive changing social and environmental conditions while retaining their strong ancestral legacy. Paleo-Indian stone tools from 5000 BCE have been unearthed throughout the state, and sophisticated copper implements slightly later in date have been collected in northern Wisconsin.

The "Woodland Tradition" (700 BCE to ca. 1300 CE) was the first culture to make pottery, domesticate plants, and build earthen burial mounds in Wisconsin. Between 600 and 900 CE, they adopted the bow and arrow, began raising corn, and buried their dead in effigy mounds that resembled birds, mammals, or people.

WHi Image ID 7790

A cliff in the driftless region

The effigy mound builders usually laid their dead in small pits or on carefully prepared surfaces, with the mounds built over them like grave markers. Sometimes the graves included an object such as a cooking pot or an arrow, but more often they contained no goods at all.

Some archaeologists and Native Americans believe that the effigy mounds symbolized spirits of the sky, earth, and water: each mound group was a picture of the Late Woodland universe, sculpted out of earth. Many of the animals depicted in the mounds were associated

An 1838 diagram of Indian effigy mounds near Blue Mounds

with important clans or groups of related families. These clans may have existed a thousand years ago. By building the mounds together, these mobile and sometimes scattered communities reinforced their social and religious ties.

About 1000 CE, people from the vicinity of present-day St. Louis moved to Wisconsin, forming the "Mississippian Culture." They came from a very different cultural background than the effigy mound builders. The Mississippian Culture lasted roughly from 1000 to 1200 CE in Wisconsin. The Mississippians traded pottery and other goods throughout the Mississippi Valley; at Aztalan in Jefferson County and near the city of Trempealeau, they built fortified

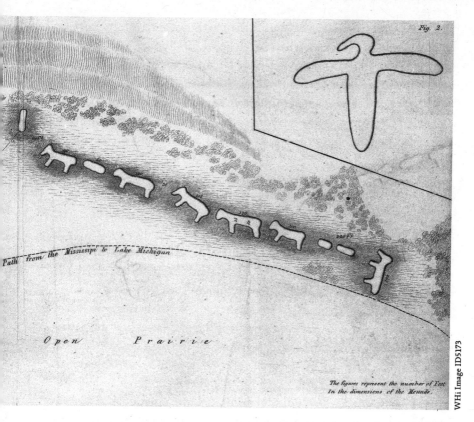

Fig. 2.

Path from the Mississipi to Lake Michigan

Open Prairie

The figures represent the number of Feet
In the dimensions of the Mounds

towns consisting of an open plaza surrounded by platforms and enclosed within a wooden palisade. Although not everyone settled into semipermanent villages at first, the presence of even a few settled villages created difficulty for mobile neighbors. Unable to pass freely from place to place, mobile groups had to choose between fighting, moving, or settling down themselves. Evidence suggests that conflict increased: some human bones dating to this period have been found embedded with projectile points and marked by stone knives.

Creating palisades and more permanent housing required substantial cooperative effort. More labor was also devoted to corn horticulture for feeding growing populations. Between 900 and 1000 CE some communities began to sculpt the earth not into effigy mounds but into ridged fields or garden beds. Food production, home building, and community improvement all tended to discourage mobility. People were reluctant to leave an established village and start all over again in a new location unless forced to do so. Formal village cemeteries replaced effigy mounds, and the Effigy Mounds Culture gradually transformed to accommodate its new social and economic environment.

But even as the culture disappeared, the mounds remained, puzzling early white settlers, who were reluctant to accept that American Indians were their creators. For most of the nineteenth century, the question of who built the mounds was debated in the press with more energy than rational judgment. An unidentified Mormon writer, for example, proposed in 1845 that the mounds had been built by people who would eventually move on to Mexico and establish the Olmec civilization. In the late 1840s, Wisconsin scientist Increase Lapham spent several years mapping and investigating effigy mounds for a monograph issued by the Smithsonian Institution. Finally, in 1894, an exhaustive survey proved beyond reasonable doubt that earlier Native Americans were indeed the people who had created the mounds, though doubters remained (for instance, an article on the "vanished race of mound builders" appeared in a Madison newspaper in 1906).

The Mississippian people left Wisconsin about 1200, succeeded by a culture known as the Oneota, believed by scholars to be the direct predecessor of today's Indian nations. The Menominee, Ho-Chunk, and Dakota (Eastern Sioux) appear to be descendants of the Oneota and were already here when other tribes arrived in the region. The earliest of these migrating tribes were the Ojibwe (Chippewa), who came to Lake Superior from the eastern Great Lakes about 1500. In the mid-1600s, warfare with the Iroquois Confederacy over fur pushed the Sauk, Meskwaki (Fox), Potawatomi, Mascouten, Kickapoo, Ottawa, Miami, and Huron into Wisconsin from their homelands in Ontario, New York, Ohio, and Michigan.

The arrival of these new tribes strained the resources available to the Menominee, Ho-Chunk, and Ojibwe. Competition for food and furs caused frequent combat and shifting alliances among the tribes. The arrival, in the seventeenth century, of white Europeans— bringing war, disease, and new technology would further transform these traditional cultures within roughly fifty years, from 1640 to 1690.

2

FORTUNES
MADE OF FUR

EARLY EXPLORERS

WHEN FRENCH AND ENGLISH OFFICIALS saw Spanish ships returning from the Americas filled with gold, they too wanted riches from the New World. Within a generation of Columbus's 1492 voyage, both countries were exploring the northern reaches of the continent. Later, at about the same time as the Pilgrims stepped ashore in Massachusetts in 1620, French explorer Étienne Brûlé is believed to have skirted the shore of Lake Superior (1622–23). He left no record of his trip, however, so the distinction of being "first European explorer" in Wisconsin usually goes to Jean Nicolet. An interpreter for Samuel de Champlain, the governor of New France, Nicolet had, like Brûlé, been sent west in search of a water route to the Pacific. In 1634 Nicolet landed at Red Banks, near Green Bay, where he met the Ho-Chunk. He did not find a route to the Pacific, but he did find a very rich source of furs. The French could make a handsome profit off the furs obtained from the Ho-Chunk if they could be brought back to Montreal for shipment to France. There, the furs would be made into the finest beaver hats. Further contact with the Ho-Chunk was prevented, though, by the Iroquois attacks of the mid-seventeenth century, which pinned the French in Montreal and Quebec and drove their potential Indian trading partners west of Lake Michigan.

When hostilities had ceased, more than twenty years after Nicolet landed, Europeans returned to Wisconsin. Explorer Médard Chouart Des Groseilliers and his partner, long believed to be his brother-in-law Pierre-Esprit Radisson, spent 1654–55 in Green Bay. They returned to Montreal in 1656 with a flotilla of Indian canoes loaded with furs, having fought their way through Iroquois attacks both coming and going. On their second voyage to the Chequamegon region of Lake Superior, in 1659–60, Des Groseilliers and Radisson built the first French fort in Wisconsin near Ashland. (Unprepared for the difficult conditions on the Wisconsin frontier, they also nearly starved to death on the headwaters of the Chippewa River.)

MISSIONARIES AND TRADERS

Furs were not the only prize to be had in North America. The quest for Indian souls also brought missionaries. The first Jesuit missionary, Father René Menard, arrived in Wisconsin in 1660, wintering on Keweenaw Bay in Michigan's Upper Peninsula and setting out in the spring for a village of exiled Hurons near the headwaters of the Black River, northwest of modern Wausau.

Some missionaries and traders formed close working relationships on the Wisconsin frontier. For example, Radisson and Des Groseilliers had returned to Montreal not only with furs but with news of a great south-flowing river—a potential new trade route to the Gulf of Mexico and the Caribbean, where the French also had settlements. This inspired the explorer René Robert Cavelier La Salle to send teenaged interpreter Louis Joliet and Jesuit priest Jacques Marquette to investigate in 1673. The coupling of God and mammon would not last, though. The Jesuits, who opposed the excesses of the fur trade, including drinking and carousing with Indian women, were expelled in the early 1700s, and the French soldiers, who guarded the lucrative Wisconsin trade routes, held power until late in the century.

Marquette and Joliet crossed Wisconsin in the summer of 1673 in search of the great river. When they stopped to consult with the

Menominee Indians about their plans, the Indians did their best to dissuade them. According to Marquette's May 1673 journal entry, the Indians warned that "the great river was full of horrible monsters, which devoured men and canoes together; that there was even a demon, who was heard from a great distance, who barred the way, and swallowed up all who ventured to approach him." Undeterred, Marquette and Joliet pressed on, traveling thousands of miles into the North American interior and confirming that the river Des Groseilliers and Radisson had first reported did indeed drain into the Gulf of Mexico. Marquette's journal, which described many of Wisconsin's natural features and Indian inhabitants, includes the first use of the word *Wisconsin,* which he transcribed as *Mescousing.* Historians have puzzled over its meaning for years. The most authoritative study of the name concluded that it was the French version of a Miami Indian word for the Wisconsin River and likely meant "river running through a red place"—probably a reference to the red sandstone that characterizes much of the river's shoreline.

BEAVER TRADE

From 1650 to 1850, Wisconsin's economy revolved around fur. Before the French traders arrived, Wisconsin's most valuable animals were white-tailed deer, catfish, wild turkey, and freshwater mussels. They had supported human communities here for twelve thousand years. But after 1650 beaver was king.

Waterproof beaver skins could be pressed into felt for hats that kept the wearer both warm and dry. From Moscow to Rome, the demand for beaver hats remained high for more than two hundred years. Those who could supply beaver pelts stood to grow rich. Merchants in Montreal shipped anything Indians would buy and demanded beaver skins in return. Trade goods included metal knives, awls and kettles, steel flints for starting fires, guns and ammunition, alcohol (which, though officially prohibited, was supplied steadily through the black market), woven woolen blankets, and porcelain beads for jewelry. These trade goods would be shipped into the interior for storage in regional warehouses in settlements such as Michilimackinac (present-day Mackinaw, Michigan), on the strait between Lakes Huron and Michigan, and then redistributed to smaller trading posts at Green Bay, Prairie du Chien, and La Pointe on Madeline Island.

In the fall, traders would advance guns, ammunition, and other supplies to Indian hunters on credit, and in the spring the hunters would return to pay off their bills in furs—a system that kept most Indian hunters in permanent debt to their French employers. The traders would pack large canoes with thousands of pounds of pelts for the trip back to Montreal, and beavers caught in Milwaukee or Minocqua would end up on the heads of customers in Paris or London. Military garrisons were established throughout the Great Lakes to make sure that trade goods came in and pelts went out with as little interruption as possible.

First Frame Building.

WHi Image ID 4714

Solomon Juneau, Milwaukee's first mayor, ran this fur trading post in Milwaukee in the 1830s.

WILD RICE

In addition to fur, wild rice was a valuable item for barter. Indians have harvested rice in Wisconsin for hundreds of years. It was an immensely important commodity, particularly for the Ojibwe and Menominee who lived in the areas where it grew. The Menominee even took their name from the Indian word for wild rice (*manomin*) and were often referred to as the "Wild Rice People" by Europeans. Traders, explorers, and missionaries valued wild rice because it was a compact and nutritious food source for long trips in the Wisconsin interior. The virtual imperishability of wild rice helped the Indians stave off famine during the long winters.

Wild rice differs from true rice—it is actually a cereal grass, like wheat, that grows in shallow lakes and streams. Before Indian life had been transformed by white settlement, the fur trade, and land cessions, entire communities would move to the lakeshore in time for the fall wild rice harvest. Each family worked in a group. A man poled two women out to the family's section of the lake in a canoe. There the women, armed with two sticks, would bend the rice stalks over the canoe and knock off kernels until the canoe was full. On shore, the rice was dried in the sun or parched over low fires. After it was dried, it would be bounced—what some called "dancing the rice"—to separate the kernel from the hull. Finally it was tossed higher in the air: the wind took the lighter chaff, while the people caught the rice in wide, flattish baskets.

Though wild rice is now considered an unpredictable crop due to its susceptibility to frost, high water, disease, and insects, Wisconsin's grain fields were once so abundant that they posed navigational problems for early European explorers—the wild rice stalks can grow as high as seven feet above the water. Little wonder, then, that Father Marquette hired guides to lead his expedition through the upper Fox River in 1673.

As a staple of the Indian diet, wild rice also provoked inter-tribal warfare, as various communities fought to protect territory containing prolific stands of rice. The Sioux of northeastern Minnesota and the Great Lakes Ojibwe bands battled for more than a century over access to the rich wild rice territories of northern Wisconsin. In one such battle, which occurred in 1806 at Mole Lake, in Forest County, between the (victorious) Sokaogon band of Ojibwe and the Sioux, nearly five hundred people were killed.

By the 1720s a chain of French trading posts arced across the interior of the continent from Montreal through the Great Lakes and down the Mississippi past St. Louis to New Orleans. Wisconsin sat directly in the center, a major conduit for the wealth of the Mississippi Valley to flow toward Quebec. The river route from Prairie du Chien up the Wisconsin River to Portage and then down the Fox River through present-day Oshkosh, Neenah, and Appleton to Green Bay was the interstate highway of the seventeenth and eighteenth centuries.

ATTACKS, RETRIBUTION, AND SHIFTING ALLIANCES

For most of the eighteenth century, the tributaries of Lakes Michigan and Superior, especially in Wisconsin, Minnesota, and western Ontario, supplied the furs that made Europeans rich. The interior fur trade was so profitable that the English tried to win Indian suppliers away from the French. The result was clandestine attacks, retribution, open warfare, and a tangle of shifting alliances. From 1700 to 1730, the Meskwaki (Fox) and the Mascouten were in open rebellion against the French, who showed little mercy in suppressing their adversaries. In 1712, for example, the French killed nearly fifteen hundred members of these tribes during the siege of Detroit alone.

Between 1755 and 1763, the French and English fought pitched battles from Pennsylvania to Quebec. These battles decided the fate of the continent. In 1755 Wisconsin's first permanent white settler, Charles de Langlade, led Great Lakes warriors against the British (including a young officer named George Washington) on the site of present-day Pittsburgh. In the end, the French lost when Montreal fell to the British in 1760. The resulting chaos helped the Ottawa chief Pontiac to unite tribes from Kentucky to Wisconsin in a campaign aimed at driving all white governments back to the Atlantic. English troops newly arrived in Green Bay, Detroit, Mackinaw, and other western posts were surrounded by thousands of Pontiac's warriors and captured or killed. Most Wisconsin tribes remained neutral, however, though the Wisconsin Ojibwe backed Pontiac and engineered the successful sneak attack on Fort Mackinaw. Peace was finally declared in 1763 and English was spoken in "Ouisconsin" for the first time.

Scottish fur trader Alexander Henry was one of the first Britons to visit Wisconsin. His 1765–66 account of the Ojibwe shows the effect of a century of colonialism on a proud and independent nation. Arriving at an Ojibwe village near Chequamegon Bay, Henry found "fifty lodges of Indians there. These people were almost naked, their trade having been interrupted, first by the English invasion of Canada and next by Pontiac's war." The men told Henry that unless they received goods on credit, their wives and children would surely perish.

Several Wisconsin tribes—such as the once-powerful Ho-Chunk and Meskwaki—had been reduced to tiny fractions of their precontact size. In nearly all Indian communities, material life, gender roles, religious practice, daily tasks, and social structure had all changed. Stable agricultural communities broke apart, as people who for hundreds of years had engaged only in seasonal hunting now became full-time hunters and wandered far and wide in pursuit of beaver. Indian women, the elderly, and children clustered around trading posts, where they caught European diseases and were often exploited. Epidemics were reported among large groups of Indians who came together to trade in 1666, 1676, 1683, 1701, 1757, 1762, and 1783. Indians and Europeans also created families together, generating a mixed-race class of offspring known as métis that blurred the lines between French, British, and Indian families.

For the British, who controlled the trade even after the American Revolution, Wisconsin Indian hunters provided a major source of income: in 1767 a third of Mackinac furs came through Green Bay. The trade thrived for a generation, and new outlets sprang up around Wisconsin (the first white settlement at Milwaukee was a tiny fur trade post started in 1795 by Jacques Vieau). Overhunting, however, gradually caused the fur trade to shift farther west, and by 1840 most furs were being shipped either from Hudson Bay to London or from Oregon to New York by sea. Wisconsin's fur trade era was over.

FROM TERRITORY
TO STATEHOOD

WHEN THE FLEDGLING UNITED STATES took legal possession of the Wisconsin Territory at the close of the Revolutionary War in 1783, hardly anyone seemed to care. The new government had more important priorities than the remote Wisconsin frontier. The area's few white residents spoke little if any English and looked not to Philadelphia and Boston for role models but to Montreal and Paris. The vast majority of Wisconsin residents were Native Americans, who needed good relations with both English and American fur companies to survive.

The creation of the United States did have one effect on Wisconsin—or at least laid the groundwork for the future Wisconsin. Before the ink had even dried on the U.S. Constitution, representatives of the thirteen states tried to figure out how new states might be added to their union. As a result, the Second Continental Congress adopted the Ordinance of 1787, commonly called the Northwest Ordinance (the Midwest was then known as the Northwest).

THE NORTHWEST ORDINANCE

The Northwest Ordinance facilitated expansion chiefly in four ways. First, it authorized a provisional government for the vast territory northwest of the Ohio River that the United States had obtained at the end of the Revolutionary War. Second, it detailed a method for making new governments out of that territory—the rules under which the Wisconsin Territory would be formed almost fifty years later, in 1836. Third, it guaranteed a bill of rights to inhabitants of the new territories and prohibited slavery in them. Finally, it out-lined a way to survey and denote the new lands so that they could be sold to settlers. This last provision was probably drafted by Nathan Dane (for whom Dane County was named) and Rufus King, although it followed fairly closely a system proposed by Thomas Jefferson three years earlier. It would profoundly influence Wisconsin settle-ment patterns. Although the survey of the territory began only in 1832, the 1787 rules provided the guidelines.

The survey provision called for teams of surveyors to hike across the land, measuring it into six-mile squares as they walked. These squares, called townships, were counted westward from a point on the Ohio/Pennsylvania border. The surveyors then subdivided each township into thirty-six one-mile-square sections, and then divided each of those into four 640-acre quarter sections, and so on, dividing and dividing the land down to the lot where your house sits. The sur-veyors would keep notes on the main features of each section. These notebooks were used to draw township maps, which would be kept in local land offices to help sell the land to new owners.

THE WAR OF 1812

In 1812 the United States declared war on Great Britain and few Wisconsin residents paid any more attention than they had in 1776. But when hostilities erupted and the British captured Mackinac Island on the straits separating lakes Huron and Michigan, both In-dians and frontier settlers chose sides. As a general rule, Wisconsin's French residents and Indians usually sided with the British rather than the Americans, though many struggled to remain neutral. Sup-port for the United States tended to come from the few American traders who had straggled up the Mississippi River from Illinois and St. Louis.

Those traders were led by William Clark, U.S. Superintendent
of Indian affairs at St. Louis and co-commander of the Lewis and
Clark Expedition of 1804–06. Hoping to keep the upper Mississippi
fur trade out of British hands, in 1814 Clark and his crew built Fort
Shelby on St. Feriole Island at Prairie du Chien. Fort Shelby would
be the site of Wisconsin's sole participation in the war of 1812. On
July 17, 1814, about sixty American soldiers were inside the fort
when the British arrived from Mackinac via Green Bay. The British
attacked with a force of about 150 regulars and four hundred Indians. For several days, the two sides half-heartedly tried to keep beyond reach of each other's guns, until the British managed to take
the sole American gunboat out of action and lay siege to Fort Shelby.
The Americans capitulated on August 9. On August 20, the British
moved in and renamed their captured prize Fort McKay. The fort
remained in British hands for only a few months, however, until December 1814, when both sides agreed to the restoration of territory
captured from the other. Prior to withdrawing from the Northwest
in 1815, retreating British forces burned the fort.

For Wisconsin, the most important legacy of the War of 1812
was the American realization that the northwestern frontier and
its fur trade needed protection. As a result, over the following decades the government established a series of military outposts that
stretched from Canada to the Gulf Coast. Three forts were constructed in Wisconsin: Fort Howard (1816–53) at Green Bay; Fort
Winnebago (1828–53) at Portage; and Fort Crawford (1816–56) at
Prairie du Chien. Besides offering protection to settlers, these early
military posts sponsored much civilian activity. Many enlisted men
found themselves building roads, constructing bridges, farming produce, cutting lumber, surveying town lots, or escorting travelers. The
forts also served as political and judicial centers, and the presence of
the military, particularly the officers and their families, helped set
the social tone of the early settlements by promoting education and
Christian religion and by hosting social gatherings for soldiers, traders, and settlers.

NATIVE AMERICANS
AND THE U.S. GOVERNMENT

To Native Americans, the forts represented both commercial opportunities and military oppression. To the frontier French, some of whom had been in place for several generations, the posts were unwelcome intrusions that brought military commanders and settlers hostile to French land claims and customs. To Yankees and Southerners relocating westward, the forts were cherished bastions of civilization in an unfamiliar wilderness.

In addition to the U.S. military, American explorers were also afoot in Wisconsin in the early nineteenth century. Major Zebulon Pike passed through Wisconsin on his 1805 trip to find the source of the Mississippi. Fifteen years later, another expedition set out for the same destination by way of Detroit, hugging Lake Superior's shore. Michigan territorial governor Lewis Cass set out with scientist Henry Schoolcraft and young James Doty (the future second territorial governor and architect of Madison's selection as capital) as secretary. They also intended to assess the condition of the Ojibwe Indians and investigate the reported mineral deposits on the Keweenaw Peninsula of upper Michigan.

Mineral wealth in the southwestern part of Wisconsin was luring thousands of people up the Mississippi River into Grant, Crawford, Iowa, and Lafayette counties. In 1822 the federal government began issuing licenses to mine in southwestern Wisconsin on land they believed had been ceded by the Sauk Indians in an 1804 treaty made in St. Louis. In the 1820s, as it became clear that the land contained significant mineral wealth, U.S. officials hurried to wrest control of the area from its native inhabitants.

In August of 1825 thousands of Indians from Wisconsin tribes gathered in Prairie du Chien. Territorial governors William Clark of Missouri and Lewis Cass of Michigan facilitated discussions that produced a general treaty of peace among all the tribes. Although it granted no land to the United States, the treaty of 1825 opened the doors for talks with individual tribes—talks that were intended to take control of Indian land. Between 1829 and 1833, the first four of these talks transferred U.S. title to all lands south of the Fox-Wisconsin waterway, and in five more councils over the next fifteen years the tribes ceded nearly all of the rest of Wisconsin to the U.S. government. Most tribes were coerced to move to new lands west of the Mississippi or confined to reservations. In a single generation, under the pressure of overwhelming military force, people who had inhabited the area for centuries or millennia lost all rights to their native lands.

More than seventy treaties were negotiated with Wisconsin Indians between 1804 and 1854. Though white negotiators always granted compensation for ceded territory, they took advantage of their Indian counterparts, and the compensation was often minimal. "We are ignorant of the way you measure land," said a Menominee chief during the negotiations at a council in Green Bay in October and November 1832. "We do not know what you mean by the acres you speak of. What is it?" U.S. negotiators could be equally ignorant: they negotiated and signed more than one treaty with Indians who lacked authority to speak for their nation.

The most dramatic event in the process of treaty and deal making came in 1832, when a portion of the Sauk Indians who resisted removal were met by an overwhelming and unmerciful military machine. An 1804 treaty negotiated in St. Louis had led government officials to believe that they had secured the right to open Sauk lands east of the Mississippi to settlement for a mere $2,500. Chief Black Hawk (Ma-ka-tai-me-she-kia-kiak) and a substantial portion of the community, on the other hand, considered the 1804 treaty invalid, believing that the two negotiators had never had the authority to speak for the whole nation. The Indians, therefore, continued to inhabit their village of Saukenuk near the mouth of the Rock River, where they had lived since the mid-eighteenth century.

A quarter century later, lead was being profitably mined in the Rock River region, and thousands of settlers were swarming to the region without regard for treaties or the land's original owners. Keokuk—another Sauk chief and Black Hawk's principal rival— along with other Sauk leaders thought it was futile to resist the massive white military force. They had complied with an 1829 government order to move across the Mississippi in return for enough corn to get through the winter. But when the government failed to honor its promises concerning this move, a group of about 1,200 Sauk who favored resistance turned to Black Hawk as their leader and returned to the Illinois side of the river in 1832, planning to reoccupy their homeland and harvest their corn.

There, Black Hawk's band was met by the Illinois militia. The Sauk fled east up the Rock River valley. Throughout that summer, Black Hawk's warriors tried to hold off the soldiers while leading their people back to the Mississippi. During their retreat, several attempts to surrender were ignored or misinterpreted, and supplies of food and water repeatedly ran out. Many very young and very old people died of hunger, thirst, or exhaustion. Warriors skirmished with the Wisconsin militia just often enough to keep them at bay, but these engagements also kindled fear in the hearts of settlers and a desire for revenge in the minds of soldiers.

At the urging of her husband, Colonel Charles Bracken, during the Black Hawk War, Sarah Bracken had fled her home in Wisconsin for the safety of Cynthiana, Kentucky. In a letter to her niece on July 21, 1832, Bracken wrote, "The country is in a dreadful situation, no business of any kind going on, no crops making the people all in Garrison, a great many murders perpetrated, and distress of every kind that can be imagined . . . I have heard from there since the army was on the march in great number and I hope will scare the savages out of the country with out any more bloodshed."

Finally, on August 1, 1832, the surviving Sauk reached the Mississippi at the mouth of the Bad Axe River, below La Crosse. Rather than crossing to safety, however, they flew one final surrender flag. The Americans rejected it, leaving the Sauk warriors caught between a gunboat in the river and pursuing troops on the bluffs. The next day, in the cruelly misnamed Battle of Bad Axe, the soldiers massacred most of the surviving men, women, and children. The gunboat fired indiscriminately on defenseless swimmers as they attempted to retreat, until the Mississippi ran red with blood. Small scattered groups, including Black Hawk, hid after the battle in the wilderness or in hunting camps of sympathetic Ho-Chunk. After the rebuke of his council on the night of Au-

WHi Image ID 11706

Robert M. Sully portrait of Black Hawk

gust 1, Black Hawk left his followers and surrendered to authorities at Fort Crawford. Of the twelve hundred people who had crossed the river with Black Hawk in April, only about 150 survived.

The message was clear to other Indian leaders: refusal to accept U.S. terms would lead to slaughter. With this sword dangling over their heads, the Ho-Chunk, Sauk, Fox, Potawatomi, and Ottawa soon gave up their lands east of the Mississippi and left the state (though many Ho-Chunk and Potawatomi later returned). By 1840 most of Wisconsin belonged to the United States rather than to its original inhabitants. The Menominee had already given up much of their territory to the Oneida, Munsee, Brothertown, and Stockbridge nations, which had relocated to Wisconsin from their homelands back east in the 1820s. In 1854 the Lake Superior Ojibwe bands ceded ownership of the northern forests (but retained rights to hunt and fish in them forever) and U.S. control over Wisconsin was complete. In his 1833 autobiography, *Life of Ma-ka-tai-me-she-kia-kiak or Black Hawk*, Black Hawk admonished, "Rock River was a beautiful country. I loved my towns, my cornfields, and the home of my people. I fought for it. It is now yours. Keep it as we did."

A NEW TERRITORY

White settlers rushed onto land left vacant by Indian removals. Wisconsin's population in 1820 was estimated at 1,444. From 1788 to 1800 Wisconsin had been part of the original Northwest Territory. Thereafter it was considered part of Indiana Territory (1800–09), Illinois (1809–18), and Michigan Territory (1818–36). New territories were created from old and the most populous ones became states. By 1836 Wisconsin's population had passed 10,000, making it eligible for its own government.

James Duane Doty, a land speculator who was then Wisconsin's representative in the Michigan legislature, led the effort to make Wisconsin a territory in its own right. On July 4, 1836, the Wisconsin Territory was born. The act of Congress creating it permitted only free white males to vote or hold territorial office. President Andrew Jackson appointed Henry Dodge governor, with responsibility to conduct a census, hold elections, and convene a territorial legislature.

Dodge acted quickly to organize the new territory's political machinery. The first census was taken in August 1836 and found only 11,683 non-Indian residents between Lake Michigan and the Dakotas. Elections were held on October 10 to choose delegates to a territorial convention. That meeting opened on October 25, 1836, in a chilly wood-framed building at Belmont, in the lead-mining region, the most populated area of the state at the time. Among the delegates' first actions was choosing a capital.

Doty, meanwhile, had traveled to the land office in Green Bay in April 1836 and, with a partner, purchased the 1,000 acres where downtown Madison now stands. He soon found a third partner, who put in another 360 acres, and the trio formed a corporation with 24 shares worth $100 each. On his way to Belmont that fall, Doty engaged surveyor John Suydam to quickly assess the site and map out a hypothetical city. If the territorial delegates chose it for the capital, Doty and his partners would earn a windfall by selling town lots to settlers and speculators.

WHi Image ID 10476

Wisconsin's Territorial Legislature met in this building in Belmont in 1836.

On November 23, 1836, the delegates began to debate nineteen possible sites, each of which had advocates like Doty who hoped to get rich quickly. Doty lobbied aggressively for votes, however—even sending a wagon to Dubuque to fetch buffalo robes that he then handed out to the freezing legislators—and apparently promising choice Madison lots to undecided voters at discount prices. Madison's uncontroversial location and Doty and Suydam's attractive map of a modern city (named for a much-admired founding father who had just died) also helped attract votes. When the dust settled on November 28, the territorial legislature had chosen Madison for its capital.

Government surveyors had already laid out the township and section lines, but now the city proper had to be laid out. For this, Doty hired a young New Yorker named Franklin Hatheway, and in the summer of 1837 the city began to take shape on an isthmus between two lakes. The capitol grounds were established atop its highest hill, major streets were laid out, buildings were erected, and

Doty drew this promotional map to convince the territorial legislature to make Madison the capital city of Wisconsin.

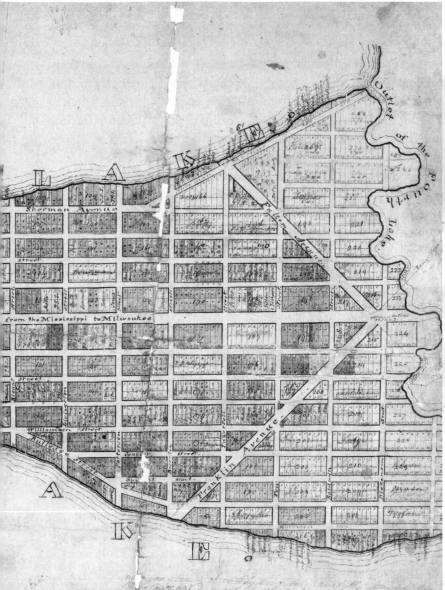

speculators as far away as New York and Washington bought lots. On their investment of $2,400, Doty and his two partners ultimately brought in $35,510.

Over the next decade the Indian tribes in Wisconsin continued to cede land, which the U.S. government surveyed. Farmers from eastern states and immigrants from Europe swarmed onto it in search of a better life. Territorial governors appointed in Washington (including Doty, Wisconsin's second territorial governor) and legislators elected by residents were kept busy authorizing road and canal companies, overseeing new banks and private corporations, and chartering public improvements. The population exploded from 11,683 in 1836 to 155,277 in 1846, enough for Wisconsin to meet the minimum requirement for statehood—60,000 free inhabitants—suggested by the Northwest Ordinance of 1787.

Political leaders and businessmen, often one and the same, had been pushing for statehood for most of Wisconsin's territorial existence. Statehood would give politicians both personal and political benefits by increasing their scope of power and influence. Businessmen would benefit from a more efficient and cohesive government, which could more effectively attract investments to aid Wisconsin's economic development. But statehood would be more difficult to achieve than anyone imagined.

STATEHOOD

The first four attempts at statehood were defeated. Finally, in 1846, a strongly Democratic territorial legislature under Governor Henry Dodge pushed through a referendum that received overwhelming majority support. While Wisconsin seemed set for a quick transition to statehood, the process of drafting and ratifying a state constitution soon proved unexpectedly complicated.

In the fall of 1846, 124 elected delegates met in Madison to prepare a constitution. Though most of the delegates were Democrats, they consisted of several warring factions that argued for ten weeks before finally agreeing on a draft. Convention delegates focused on the economic and social problems of the time, especially those having to do with banks and paper money. Influenced by President Jackson's conviction that coinage rather than paper money was the only safe currency and the popular idea that legislatures were easily bribed by banks, anti-bank delegate Edward G. Ryan of Racine drafted an article that effectively prohibited all commercial banking in Wisconsin. Ryan's proposal forbade the legislature from creating or authorizing banks, banned all banking-related activities, and allowed the circulation of paper money only in denominations less than twenty dollars. Ryan's article passed by a vote of 79 to 27.

The convention concluded in December of 1846. Far more advanced and progressive than other states', Wisconsin's proposed constitution included a number of controversial articles besides that on banking. The 1846 constitution allowed immigrants who applied for citizenship to vote (in many other states property ownership, not just citizenship, was a requirement to vote), granted married women the right to own property (women were often considered property themselves in other states), and (perhaps most significantly, and despite strong objections from politicians) made the question of black suffrage subject to popular referendum.

These provisions excited spirited debate. Racine attorney Marshall Strong thought Wisconsin had gone mad. Objecting to the terms allowing women to own property, Strong lamented during the debates, "When the husband returns at night, perplexed with care, dejected with anxiety, depressed in hope, will he find . . . the same nice and delicate appreciation of his feelings he has heretofore found? Will her welfare, and feelings, and thoughts, and interests be all wrapped up in his happiness, as they now are? . . . The effect of this law upon the husband, upon the wife, upon the children, and upon all the domestic relations will be most fearful." Few citizens were satisfied with the entire draft of the constitution. Each region of the territory reacted differently to these issues, but enough opposition surfaced to defeat the constitution and black suffrage in April 1847.

A new convention met in December 1847 and drafted a more widely acceptable and moderate constitution in only seven weeks. Using the results of the April vote to guide them, the delegates prepared a document that omitted any mention of women's property rights or black suffrage. Suffrage was given to white native-born men, immigrant men who had declared their intention to become citizens, and Indians who had been declared U.S. citizens. The legislature would also be allowed to charter banks after submitting the matter to popular vote. Wisconsin voters accepted the new constitution in March of 1848, and on May 29, 1848, Wisconsin became the thirtieth state.

4

CALLING
WISCONSIN HOME

"Wisconsin is most favorably situated not only for agriculture, but also for manufacturing and commerce. Nearly all her
territory lies in the Mississippi Valley, which is the garden spot of
the world," proclaimed the popular guidebook *Northern Wisconsin: A
Hand-Book for the Homeseeker*. Albert G. Tuttle, who had come west
from Connecticut in the 1840s to investigate Wisconsin, concurred
in a series of letters to his wife in 1847: "The natural resources of
Wisconsin are almost unlimited and nothing is wanted but the
hand of cultivation to make it the garden of the world." He finished,
"There is a softness and beauty in the landscape which is indescrib-
able and which the hand of art will fail to improve." How could anyone resist?

IMMIGRATION

Clearly many could not. Between 1836 and 1860, people flooded into
Wisconsin: the population increased from 11,000 to 775,881. Some of
these settlers came from the eastern United States; others came from
Europe. The first immigrants tended to settle in the southern parts
of Wisconsin. Economic and social changes in Europe, coupled with
natural disasters such as the potato blight in Ireland, had increased
many Europeans' discontent and desire to emigrate. Writer and social reformer Margaret Fuller visited Milwaukee in 1843 and could

hardly miss the city's explosive growth. "The torrent of emigration swells very strongly towards this place. During the fine weather, the poor refugees arrive daily in their national dresses all travel-soiled and worn," she wrote. "Here, on the pier, I see disembarking the Germans, the Norwegians, the Swedes, the Swiss." By 1850 one-third of the state's population was foreign-born.

Of the more than 100,000 foreign-born Wisconsinites in 1850, only 48,000 could claim English as their native language. Nearly one-half of these English speakers were Irish. Of the non-English-speaking immigrants, the Germans were by far the most numerous. Nearly 40 percent of Milwaukee's population was German-born; with them came beer gardens, shops with German signs and German goods, German foods, and authentic German culture. Norwegians constituted the second largest group, followed closely by Canadians of primarily French descent.

Between 1852 and 1855 the Wisconsin Commission of Emigration actively encouraged the settlement of European immigrants in Wisconsin. Immigrants were seen as the fuel for the state's growth. The Commission published pamphlets extolling the state's virtues in German, Norwegian, Dutch, and English and distributed them throughout Europe as well as in eastern port cities. Advertisements encouraging people to come west also appeared in more than nine hundred newspapers. However, in 1855 rising antiforeign sentiment, primarily directed at Irish Catholics, led to the dissolution of the Commission.

The demise of the Commission did little to deter immigrants. The foreign-born population continued to increase, largely due to the propaganda produced by land speculators, who worked hard to sell their land holdings, and due to the efforts of the immigrants themselves, whose letters home encouraged friends and family to join them.

Carl de Haas helped recruit many of these immigrants. A young German schoolteacher, de Haas settled in Calumet, Wisconsin, in 1847. Impressed with what he found upon his arrival, de Haas decided to write his own guide to encourage others to immigrate to his new home. While many Europeans tended to view reports from

WHi Image ID 37967

The Siggelkow family came from Mecklenburg, Germany, and settled near Madison around 1864. This picture was taken the day before the family sailed for America.

the United States with suspicion (and rightly so, as most were advertising pitches from railroads and land companies), de Haas's *Nordamerika, Wisconsin, Calumet* was widely regarded as trustworthy. Its honest recounting of de Haas's personal experiences helped other German immigrants plan their own voyages. De Haas sensibly advised immigrants, for example, to prevent theft by keeping their eyes on their baggage until stowed by customs officials. He also recommended bringing food along for the boat ride, as most shipboard food wasn't very good.

Whether as a result of books like de Haas's, letters from family and friends, or the strongest inducement of all—land—people traveled over sea and earth to make their homes in Wisconsin. As the nineteenth century progressed, not just Irish, Germans, and Norwegians but also increasing numbers of Finns, Danes, Italians, Swedes, Belgians, Swiss, Bohemians, Czechs, and Poles called Wisconsin home.

Yankees quickly rose to dominance on the Wisconsin frontier, partly because they knew the mechanics of land surveys and sales and often had a line of credit to get them started and also because they had seen the transformation of the land from wilderness to world market many times before. Taking possession of town sites, water power, and some of the best farmlands, they became the entrepreneurs, speculators, lawyers, editors, ministers, and leading politicians. By imposing their institutions, ideas, and customs on Wisconsin, many Yankees could feel as though they had never left home.

British immigrants, particularly English and Scottish, easily assimilated into Yankee culture. Enterprising, aggressive, and relatively well educated, they were less likely to settle in ethnic enclaves and were more likely than other European immigrants to be businessmen, merchants, or other professionals. The single largest British group to come to Wisconsin, the Cornish, were an exception, settling in an ethnic island of miners in the lead region of the southwest. But with the decline of mining, the Cornish did readily assimilate to farming and other small-town occupations.

Of the English-speaking immigrants, the Irish were the most easily identified, largely because they were poor and Catholic. Unlike other immigrant groups, the Irish did not move immediately westward after arriving in the United States: the average Irish immigrant had spent seven years in the United States before moving to Wisconsin. Most Irish did not come to Wisconsin for the chance to farm; they shared the Yankee readiness to move on if the price was right or the opportunity for something better appeared. Many Irish worked in the lead region both in the mines and in support industries such as lumbering, smelting, and rail construction. Irish were to be found in nearly any town that had seen the construction of a plank road, canal, or railroad. Others settled in the southeastern counties and in the city of Milwaukee, where they worked as laborers, domestics, and artisans. Although they did not consciously settle in separate ethnic communities, they were often ghettoized in urban areas by their poverty and faith.

Like the Irish, Germans were widely dispersed, settling readily into both city and countryside across the country. Wisconsin held

Wisconsin.

Ein Bericht über

Bevölkerung, Boden, Klima, Handel

— und die —

industriellen Verhältnisse

dieses Staates im Nordwesten der nordamerika-
nischen Union,

Mit zwei Tabellen über Münzen, Maaße und Gewichte
Deutschlands und Amerika's, sowie einer Karte.

Veröffentlicht von den

Staats-Einwanderungs-Commissären.

Dritte Auflage.

1870.

Milwaukee.

Schnellpressen-Druck des „Herold."

The Wisconsin State Board of Immigration published this brochure in German to lure German immigrants. Its topics include the state's population, climate, trade, and industrial conditions.

particular appeal for its land and familiar climate. Most entered in three major waves between 1845 and 1900, spurred by political, social, and economic upheavals in Europe. The earliest groups came for largely religious and political reasons, while those who migrated after mid-century were primarily farmers, artisans, and laborers. Germans tended to settle into and form ethnic enclaves, creating schools, churches, and other community organizations based on German culture and identity.

Norwegian immigrants usually came from a farming background and, like the Germans, sought a place on the land. Highly responsive to books promoting America, most Norwegians first came to the Rock River valley of Illinois and spread northward into Wisconsin; by 1850, an astonishing 70 percent of the Norwegians in the United States were clustered in Wisconsin. Norwegians tended to settle in colonies representing their own districts and dialects. Accustomed to working hard on marginal lands, they took whatever land was left, including hills and swamps, and turned it into productive farms. Yankees tended to view Norwegians with derision, referring to them as "Scandihoovian Indians." In the territorial council, Marshall Strong declared in 1847 that "he had seen Norwegians living without what other people would have considered the most absolute necessities of life, burrowed so to say in holes in the ground, in huts dug in the banks of the earth." To Yankees, the Norwegians' chief virtue was their tendency to isolate themselves.

Europeans and Yankees were not the only people who saw their future in Wisconsin. One of the most interesting developments in the 1820s was the emigration of several Indian communities. The Stockbridge-Munsee band of Mohicans, part of the Oneida nation, and the Brothertown community (a group of Pequot, Niantic, Montauk, and other coastal peoples who'd been given refuge by the Oneida in New York) all came to Wisconsin to escape exploitation in the East. They secured land in northeastern Wisconsin from the Menominee and Ho-Chunk and established new communities on the frontier.

TRANSPORTATION

The increase in population intensified the demand for better transportation. Immigrants came to Wisconsin by ship, steamboat, railroad, horseback, and wagon. Improving transportation would help encourage the mass migration westward. Transportation routes and ease of access, particularly from the port city of Milwaukee, also often spelled success or failure for towns that were already fighting for the county courthouse, the hospital, and the state university. The opening of the Erie Canal in 1825, connecting the Great Lakes with the Atlantic Ocean, made some in Wisconsin eager for canals and harbors of their own to connect the Great Lakes with the Mississippi River.

Transporting agricultural products, people, lead, and other goods to and from lake ports offered big financial rewards to Wisconsin's settlers, businessmen, and promoters. Sending products down the Mississippi was a long and costly route, often troubled by periods of low water. Towns on the lakeshore received many new immigrants, but unimproved harbors often caused boats to bypass Wisconsin towns and continue on to Chicago. The citizens of Racine, Milwaukee, Kenosha, and other towns lobbied Congress for money to build better harbors, but their requests usually went unanswered.

Lacking both a railroad and the means to build one, a group from Green Bay proposed the construction of a portage, or passageway, between the Fox and Wisconsin rivers as an avenue of internal transport. An 1839 federal survey estimated that overcoming the serious obstacles to building a portage, including the rapids of the Fox River, would cost upwards of half a million dollars. Although the Fox River Improvement Company (as the group behind the portage plan came to be called) was granted land to sell by Congress to raise money for the project, the work progressed slowly, and in the end, the route proved too long and winding to be of much use.

At the same time, another canal was underway in Milwaukee. In 1838 Byron Kilbourne promoted the construction of a canal from Milwaukee to the Rock River to provide a continuous water route from the lead region in the southwest. The canal got no farther than some docks on the Milwaukee River before the legislature withdrew all support from the Milwaukee and Rock River Canal Company in 1841. Because competition and financial constraints severely limited the capabilities of many harbor improvement and canal construction projects, steamships on the Mississippi River and Great Lakes continued to play an important role in bringing both settlers and goods to Wisconsin.

In the late 1840s railroads eclipsed most talk of canals in Wisconsin. Railroads had proven themselves in the East, and in the early 1840s, there was already talk of uniting the Atlantic and Pacific oceans with a continental railroad. A line across Wisconsin would provide a means for moving produce, consumer goods, and people that was independent of uncertain water- and roadways. Moreover, many businessmen and officials saw railroads as a way to draw the various regions of the state together in a common interest. Railroads would also encourage and facilitate further settlement.

The opening of Illinois's Chicago–Galena railroad stirred the Wisconsin legislature into action. In 1847 the legislature authorized a line from Milwaukee to Waukesha that was later extended to the Mississippi. The first train ran from Milwaukee to Waukesha on February 25, 1851. By April of that year trains were running briskly—one passenger train and one freight train daily. Rather than waiting for a railroad to come to them, town officials in Prairie du Chien took matters into their own hands and asked the legislature to charter a line from Madison. In 1857 the first east–west railroad from Lake Michigan to the Mississippi was complete. Soon after, a line from Milwaukee to La Crosse opened, and other lines were extended north from Chicago.

Though Wisconsin did not become an important link in the Atlantic–Pacific rail system, railroads provided farmers with better prices and expanded marketing opportunities by offering a more reliable way to transport products to eastern markets—both factors told immigrants that a profitable future was possible in Wisconsin.

LEAD AND LUMBER

LEAD MINING

ALTHOUGH SOUTHWESTERN WISCONSIN is best known today for its rich farmlands, city names like New Diggings and Mineral Point evoke a time when local mines produced much of the nation's lead. In the early nineteenth century, Wisconsin lead mining was more promising and attractive to potential settlers than either farming or the waning fur trade. Its potential get-rich-quick rewards lured a steady stream of settlers up the Mississippi River, and by 1829 more than four thousand miners produced 13 million pounds of lead a year.

Europeans had known of the presence of lead ore in the upper Mississippi since the seventeenth century, and for hundreds of years before that, the Ho-Chunk, Fox, Sauk, and other Indian tribes had mined the easily accessible lead. French fur trader Nicolas Perrot began actively trading in lead mined by Indians in the 1680s, and French explorer Henri Joutel, who was in the area as early as 1687, reported in his journal, first published in Paris in 1713 as *A Journal of the Last Voyage Perform'd by Monsr. de la Sale, to the Gulph of Mexico, to Find Out the Mouth of the Missisipi River*, that "travelers who have been at the upper part of the Mississippi affirm that they have found mines of very good lead there." When the French withdrew from the area in 1763, Indians guarded the mines carefully, revealing their locations only to favored traders such as Julien Dubuque (for whom the city of Dubuque, Iowa, is named).

Settlement in the southwest remained slow until a series of treaties between 1804 and 1832 gradually ceded all Indian lands south of the Wisconsin River to the United States. An intensifying rate of settlement coincided with an increasing demand for lead, which was widely used in the manufacture of pewter, pipes, weights, paint, and, of course, ammunition for the firearms of an expanding U.S. military.

Miners who moved to the area in the 1820s and 1830s wasted little time in constructing shelters. Some simply burrowed holes into hillsides, earning miners the nickname "badgers" and the future state of Wisconsin its moniker as "the Badger State." The tools and techniques involved in lead mining in these early years were relatively simple and inexpensive, allowing lucky miners to strike it rich with little personal expense.

Luck was definitely the key to successful mining. William Davidson came to the lead-mining region around Galena in 1828 before moving north to Hazel Green, Wisconsin, to prospect at mines. "I started a prospect hole, expecting to find a mineral lode in a few days; but I found that success was not so much in hard labor, as in good luck," wrote Davidson in his *Personal narrative of experiences in the lead mining regions, 1855.* "And being a stranger, if I discovered a lode, the country was then staked off in what was called mineral lots, agreeable to the mining regulations, I would either have to fight my way through fifty claimants, or be swindled out of my prospects."

Many of the first miners came to Wisconsin from Missouri, which had experienced a similar lead boom a few years earlier. Communities sprang up quickly around the mines, as other industries and businesses were founded to serve the residents that mining attracted. In the 1830s, unemployed tin miners began arriving from Cornwall in southwestern England. The Cornish settled primarily in Mineral Point and constructed small, limestone homes similar to those they had left in England.

Miners deep in a lead mine in Cassville

ZINC, COPPER, AND IRON

The lead industry ended almost as quickly as it began, however. It peaked in the 1840s, by which time Wisconsin mines had yielded more than half the national output. But demand for Wisconsin lead was beginning to decline. Miners had exhausted the supply of easily obtainable ore, which made mining more expensive and less appealing to investors. In 1844 a third of the region's residents left for copper and iron mines elsewhere, while the discovery of gold in California caused many others to head west in 1849. For those who remained, mining often became a part-time supplement to farming. Some men began to mine for zinc, and for a few years in the late nineteenth century, Mineral Point had the largest zinc smelting facility in the world.

The decline in lead profits also induced mining experts to look north, where copper deposits had long been noted. In prehistoric times, Indians had mined copper on the shores of Lake Superior.

Between 3000 and 1200 BCE, copper jewelry and implements from Wisconsin and Upper Michigan were part of a trade network that stretched from the Rocky Mountains to the Gulf Coast, giving rise to the name "Old Copper Culture."

Easy access to copper deposits—some of them literally lying on the shore—was one of the first features early French travelers noticed about Lake Superior. Explorers such as Étienne Brûlé and Samuel Champlain and missionaries like Father Claude Allouez all mentioned the copper deposits. In 1739 French officer Louis Denis De La Ronde had attempted the first systematic mining of copper in northern Wisconsin after reporting favorably on the region's potential. Ongoing warfare between the Sioux and Ojibwe, however, dashed De La Ronde's plans. Later English-speaking travelers such as Jonathan Carver and Henry Schoolcraft also commented on the abundant mineral wealth of the region.

Nevertheless, for several more decades, northern Wisconsin remained largely untouched by white settlement, with only a few fur trading posts, lumber camps, and fledgling ports dotting its landscape. Lake Superior's iron and copper mines became more appealing to potential white settlers in the nineteenth century, particularly as the federal government pushed to remove all Indians west of the Mississippi. The Ojibwe successfully defended their homeland, though they did allow white settlers to extract its minerals while the Ojibwe retained the right to dwell, hunt, and fish in northern Wisconsin.

During the 1850s Lake Superior's iron and copper mines began to draw attention. Writing in 1855, James Gregory declared, "Iron ore of unlimited extent and of great purity may be found at Lake Superior, in the Baraboo district, and at the Iron Ridge in Dodge and Washington counties." Mining in northern Wisconsin followed a different economic and cultural trajectory than did development in the southern part of the state, however. Northern settlement was shaped largely by and for the benefit of people outside Wisconsin, especially investors from the East who hoped to make a quick fortune. Their interest in extracting and transporting ore from the western end of Lake Superior led to the founding of Superior, Ashland, and Bayfield.

Iron ore was initially smelted with locally produced charcoal, but companies soon found it more profitable to ship the ore east for refining. This required the construction of a canal at Sault Ste. Marie (opened in 1855) to connect Lake Superior to the other lakes and development of an intricate system for loading ore onto a specialized fleet of lake ships and unloading it in Chicago, Cleveland, or Pittsburgh, where it was turned into iron and steel. This kind of multistate interdependence was quite different from the decentralized farming economy of southern Wisconsin, where self-sufficient homesteaders supplied produce to their own families, local markets, and nearby urban centers.

The initial development of the Lake Superior region was brief, however, as the economic panic of 1857 and the Civil War diverted capital from northern mines. The desire for wealth that had brought capital into the Lake Superior region carried it away with equal speed. In the late 1850s, highly touted cities such as Ashland vanished almost overnight as investors and local residents sought greener pastures elsewhere.

The discovery and mapping of high-grade Bessemer ore in the Gogebic Range of northern Wisconsin and Michigan in 1872 renewed interest in the region and even led to a frenzy of speculation. Fortunes were made and lost overnight in northern Wisconsin during the 1880s. One of those who made a fortune was Morris Pratt of Rock County. He used the money he had earned from investing in the mines (on the advice of noted Wisconsin psychic Mary-Hayes Chynoweth, who also struck it rich in the Gogebics) to fund the construction of a spiritualist academy in Watertown. Mining fortunes left their marks on cities all over Wisconsin, even those like Watertown, hundreds of miles to the south of the mines.

Other newly rich locals constructed palatial homes, while wealthy investors from the East came to view the mines. Communities such as Ironwood and Hurley sprang up around mines, and travel guides praised the natural beauty of the region's lakes, rivers, and forests. The 1880s boom on the Gogebic, though at times exuberant, was not based entirely on speculation; tremendous deposits of high-grade ore were actually uncovered and successfully brought to market. But the investment in northern mining that peaked in 1886 and 1887 was soon followed by a crash that eliminated most of the smaller companies.

The riches of the Gogebic Range proved a far more sustainable and lucrative industry for towns in Michigan than for those in Wisconsin, as most of the region's profitable deposits lay across the state line. Dependence on eastern financiers and out-of-state consumers had left the region without the economic and political stability to determine its own destiny. As resources began to dwindle and out-of-state investors shifted their interest to more lucrative possibilities, capital and leadership departed from Wisconsin's northern mining towns, leaving the people who remained to survive as best they could.

Those people attracted to work in the northern mines were a distinct population. Cornish miners, some of whom had immigrated first to work the lead mines in southwestern Wisconsin, arrived early and brought their experiences in underground mining to the north. Swedes and Finns also migrated to the new towns around Lake Superior in large numbers, followed slightly later by Croats and Slovenes—ethnic groups whose languages, religions, and customs differed dramatically from the Yankee, German, and Norwegian populations in the south.

LUMBER

Unlike mining, the timber industry remained an important part of the northern Wisconsin economy and helped to offset the economic effects of the mining decline. In fact, by the late nineteenth century, Wisconsin was one of the premier lumber-producing states in the

United States, and forest products led the state's industrial economy. Forests along the Wisconsin River were the first to fall before the lumberjack's axe, and the cities of Stevens Point and Wausau sprang up to support loggers and mill workers. Rivers provided a convenient way to transport pine logs from the forests to the mills. The mills then used the same rivers to power water wheels and huge saws that cut the logs into boards—most of the major cities in central and northern Wisconsin were built on rivers.

The Wolf River in northeastern Wisconsin was a second major lumbering district. By the late 1840s it had given birth to Neenah, Oshkosh, Appleton, and other towns at the river's end. Because the Wolf ran through their reservation, the Menominee also developed a successful logging industry. Menominee men stayed in lumber camps all winter, cutting timber and hauling it by sleigh to the riverbank so it could be floated downstream when the ice broke in the spring.

The dining room at August Mason's lumber camp in Brill, Wisconsin

WHi Image ID 1961

The watersheds of the Black and Chippewa rivers in the northwest constituted the third major lumbering region. Dozens of small independent companies gradually combined into a conglomerate led by Frederick Weyerhaeuser that shipped logs and boards downriver to St. Louis, creating towns such as Eau Claire and Black River Falls in the process. From the Black River valley alone enough pine was harvested to have built a boardwalk nine feet wide and four inches thick that spanned the globe.

Unfortunately, lumbering also went hand in hand with forest fires, which were fueled, in part, by the debris left behind by the lumbermen. Logging shed sunlight on the forest floor, and this, combined with dryness and tinder, meant conditions were ripe for a spark. On October 8, 1871, fire ripped through northern Wisconsin, obliterating the towns of Peshtigo and Brussels with its hurricane-force winds. The Great Peshtigo Fire, as it came to be called, cut a swath ten miles wide and forty miles long, turning thousands of acres of white pine into a desolate wasteland. Nearly fifteen hundred people lost their lives and another fifteen hundred were seriously injured; around three thousand people were left homeless. Though the fire is mostly forgotten today—it occurred on the same day as the renowned Great Chicago Fire—the Peshtigo Fire is the most disastrous forest fire in American history.

Railroads transformed the lumber industry in the mid- to late nineteenth century. Transporting lumber by train allowed loggers to work year-round and to cut lumber that had previously been impossible to float down the river. As lumber camps moved deeper into the woods and farther from cities, camps increased in size to meet the needs of the men. Bunkhouses, a kitchen and dining hall, a company store, a blacksmith, and a carpentry shop became typical features of lumber camps. Lumberjacks slept two to a bunk, according to former lumberman Thomas McBean, each with a "pair of blankets, and their turkey (a grain sack with their extra clothing in it) for a pillow." Food, according to McBean, was "plain," consisting of bread, salt pork, beans, blackstrap molasses, potatoes, coffee and tea—"no cream or pie." And in the winter, when the pork ran out, the men ate cod from the rivers.

The soft pine forests of northern and central Wisconsin provided a seemingly endless supply of raw materials to urban markets. Products made from Wisconsin trees included doors, window sashes, furniture, beams, and ships built in lakefront industrial centers such as Sheboygan, Manitowoc, and Milwaukee. Much of the lumber was also used in buildings. The forests of nineteenth-century Wisconsin still surround us today, in the shapes of houses, schools, and churches from Milwaukee to Superior.

But what seemed endless was not. Northern forests were leveled by the disastrous practice of clear-cutting, and despite extensive efforts to settle new immigrants on the so-called cutover lands, the region's small farms, poor soil, and a short growing season conspired to keep agricultural productivity low. Northern Wisconsin did not fully recover from the effects of the lumber and mining boom and bust until the rise of tourism in the twentieth century.

WHi Image ID 57239

A team of four horses pulls a sleigh loaded with logs out of the woods.

SOCIAL and MORAL
IMPROVEMENT

LUMBERING, MINING, AND LAND SALES generated most of Wisconsin's wealth in the early years, most of which was directed toward construction, land investment, and development projects— activities that would propel the state's economic growth and, it was hoped, encourage settlement. This left few resources to develop cultural and intellectual institutions. Many of the state's early settlers nevertheless expressed an underlying concern for cultural, social, and moral improvement.

Some, particularly those from New York, New England, and French Canada, felt the need to found the same cultural institutions they had known in the East. A primary feature of this movement toward intellectual and spiritual development was an impulse to form discussion groups, libraries, and, most importantly, schools.

THE PUSH FOR EDUCATION

Wisconsin's first public schoolteacher was Electa Quinney, a member of the Stockbridge-Munsee band of Mohicans. Quinney had come to Wisconsin during the massive Indian removal from New York in 1827 and was especially interested in teaching the children of the Stockbridge-Munsee settlement around Kaukauna. In 1828 she opened the first school in the state without an enrollment fee, allowing families who had been unable to afford school fees the luxury of an education. Both whites and Indians attended her school. One of her first students, Quinney's nephew J. Quinney, reported that she was well liked and that she moved among the best circles at Fort Howard in Green Bay, teachers being held in high regard in a community with limited access to education.

Outside of Quinney's school, however, many of the New Englanders among Wisconsin's white settlers were shocked at the condition of Wisconsin's schools (or lack thereof) and ardently supported the creation of a public education system. Teachers were scarce, though, and few Wisconsin communities had schools comparable to those in parts of the East. Wisconsin's teachers were usually fresh out of school themselves and often taught several grades in crowded schoolhouses. People in Madison and Milwaukee sometimes sent their children to private schools because the public schools had no more room. Schools in the lead-mining region were so inadequate that many children attended private boarding schools in nearby states. Until statehood, financial support for territorial schools could come only through taxes, and many citizens fought hard against high taxation rates. It took time to convince people of the necessity of voluntary taxation to educate other people's children in addition to their own.

Yet at a time when few if any schools in the United States were entirely free of charge, Wisconsin's constitution was revolutionary in providing for both a state university and a system of free common schools. They were to be funded by taxes and land sales, making education widely available for children between the ages of four and twenty. Unfortunately, limited resources and money constrained school improvements until the Civil War. Though the legislature established the University of Wisconsin in 1848, classes did not meet until 1850 and the university received no state funding until 1866. Prior to statehood, the Wisconsin legislature had also incorporated four private colleges: Carroll College, Beloit College, Lawrence Institute (now Lawrence University), and Sinsinawa Mound College.

The push for education was one part of a larger movement in the nineteenth century for people to improve themselves, their communities, and their nation. Idealism and growing prosperity gave people the time to see the problems that needed to be fixed, the impulse to make changes, and the confidence to believe that they knew how best to do it.

Many reformers viewed education not just as a measure of intellectual development but also as a means of social change. As the number of immigrants continued to grow and the population became more diverse, the state launched a series of efforts to assimilate disparate immigrant groups into mainstream American culture. Learning the English language became central to these Americanization efforts, which focused on state regulation of public and private schools and would eventually reach a climax in 1890, when the state legislature enacted the Bennett Law.

In the 1880s many Yankees had begun to call for laws holding parochial schools more accountable to the government and requiring that their classes be conducted in English. Many immigrants, especially Germans, had established their own schools upon settling in Wisconsin as a way to preserve their own cultures. Yankees, however, often saw the schools as a form of unpatriotic resistance to assimilation. When William Dempster Hoard of Fort Atkinson ran for governor in 1888, the school reforms advocated by Yankees became a central theme of his successful campaign.

The following legislative session, Assemblyman Michael Bennett of Dodgeville introduced a school reform bill and Hoard's program was put into effect. The bill required stricter enforcement of attendance in both public and private schools, and specified that children could only attend parochial schools located in their public school district. Most pointedly, it also required that all schools, public and private, conduct classes in English.

German Americans denounced the Bennett Law, as it came to be called, as an assault on their culture by Yankees who sought to foist their own values on everyone else. Christian Koerner, legal editor of Milwaukee's leading German newspaper, *Germania*, published a widely distributed pamphlet outlining his objections to the law using legal and statistical evidence. "Among the inalienable rights of men which the Declaration of Independence enumerates, is the 'pursuit of happiness'. . . . But domestic happiness is sadly interfered with as soon as strangers dictate to a parent, as soon as a majority of the citizens dictates to the minority, how they shall bring up their children," Koerner wrote. "But this Bennett Law would deprive parents of their parental authority . . . would dictate to them how they shall bring up their children, and would in this manner interfere with our domestic peace and happiness."

Proponents viewed the law as a complete victory over foreign degradation of American culture. More moderate voices argued for the inevitability of assimilation, contending that learning English would not destroy German culture. Opposition to the Bennett Law was loud, persistent, and widespread, however, and in 1890, after only a single term, the Republicans and Governor Hoard were voted out of office, largely on the strength of the German vote. Though the Bennett Law was repealed the following legislative session, the controversy prompted many German schools to begin implementing bilingual instruction.

INDIAN SCHOOLS

Indians endured far worse. From the late nineteenth century through the 1920s, government-sanctioned Indian education programs energetically tried to assimilate American Indians into mainstream culture by placing them in institutions such as the Tomah Indian Industrial School, designed to replace their traditional ways with those approved by the government. White policy makers and teachers viewed their efforts as an act of kindness. To Indians, however, it often seemed an act of aggression. As one Stockbridge woman later recalled, "They tried to erase us."

Federal Indian policy called for children to be removed from their families and, in many cases, enrolled in government-run boarding schools. If kept away from the "corrupting influences" of their

WHi Image ID 25836

Oneida children in a village school around 1910, the height of the U.S. government's policy of assimilation

traditionally minded families, government officials believed, Indian children would absorb the values, knowledge, and practical skills of the dominant American culture. The federal government also established two other types of schools to educate increasing numbers of Indian children at a lower cost: the reservation boarding school and day schools. On many reservations, missionaries operated private schools that combined religion with academic training in pursuit of goals similar to those of the government Indian schools.

While the daily schedule varied at each type of Indian school, a typical day at a boarding school usually consisted of a series of tasks punctuated by the ringing of bells. Students marched from one activity to the next, with regular inspections and drills organized by age. Conformity to rules and regulations was strongly encouraged, and the curriculum emphasized vocational training. The federal Office of Indian Affairs issued manuals describing what it considered basic knowledge and skills. The 1911 manual called *Some Things that Girls Should Know How to Do and Hence Should Learn How to do in School*, for example, assumed that Indian girls would return home after school rather than work in business or industry; the manual provided lessons on cooking, sewing, and cleaning. Girls would learn how to make a cake, the art of pickling, how to make butter, and the proper use of soap and water in dish washing. Cleanliness and housekeeping received particular emphasis, because many whites believed that Indians lived in filthy, degraded conditions.

Like the Bennett Law for Germans, the foremost requirement for Indian assimilation into American society was mastery of the English language, though the punishment for noncompliance was far more severe for Indian children than for Germans. Indian children were prohibited from speaking their native language at all. Those caught doing so were often physically punished.

WHi Image ID 2105

Indian girls learning to sew at the Lac du Flambeau U.S. Government School for Indian children, around 1895

After several decades, reports on Indian education revealed glaring deficiencies, including poor diet, disease, overcrowding, excessive labor, and substandard teaching. In the 1920s, the Bureau of Indian Affairs changed its mind about boarding schools. The following decade, the policy of assimilation was officially abandoned.

SETTLEMENT HOUSES

Besides schools, efforts to assimilate Indians and immigrants to American culture came through private reform institutions known as settlement houses. Settlement houses usually focused on the needs of a particular group, often immigrants, and depended for their support on the benevolence of generous patrons. For recent immigrants, settlement house workers tried to ease the adjustment to a new country by consciously teaching white middle-class values in urban ethnic neighborhoods. Though they often betrayed a paternalistic attitude toward the poor, settlement houses also acted as advocates for immigrants, organized protective associations, sponsored festivals, and tried to preserve the cultural heritage of ethnic groups by offering them a place to eat, socialize, and take classes.

One of the most famous of these establishments was Milwaukee's The Settlement, a multipurpose reform organization aimed at Jewish immigrants, primarily Russian Orthodox. The house offered classes in history, Hebrew, and mothering, as well as athletic and cultural clubs, a library, a bank, athletic facilities, and public baths. Cooking classes, taught by the head of the organization, Milwaukee-born Lizzie Black Kander, proved among the most popular offerings and brought The Settlement lasting fame.

Kander believed that food was a powerful means of religious and cultural expression, and she used culinary reform to aid in the assimilation of immigrant girls and to introduce immigrant women to American consumer culture. In teaching modern cooking skills, Kander and the other women instructors introduced nutrition, American methods of housekeeping, and menu planning, demonstrating how

American ingredients could be incorporated into traditional Jewish dishes. The Settlement operated the only kosher kitchen outside of New York City.

Kander's personal involvement in the cooking classes led to the publication of a recipe collection in 1901. *The Settlement Cookbook: The Way to a Man's Heart* was an immediate success, combining recipes with instructions on cleanliness, food storage, and housekeeping. The book was an amalgam of Jewish and American traditions, all presented within a framework of modern domestic science. Kander served as editor of the cookbook until her death, revising and adding new recipes to each edition. The cookbook is still in print today and has sold more than 2 million copies—the most successful community cookbook ever published. Profits helped to pay for a new building in 1911 and another, five times larger, in 1931.

RELIGION

Churches offered another arena of moral and social improvement. The 1830s and 1840s were the big era of church formation in Wisconsin. An ever-growing number of towns constructed various denominational churches; Episcopal, Methodist, Baptist, Congregational, Lutheran, and Presbyterian ministers competed for members with Catholic priests who had been here since the fur trade days. Many of these churches had sent or organized missionary and benevolent societies to recruit new members, reform existing communities, or open schools in Wisconsin. Church-sponsored benevolent societies also provided middle-class white women with opportunities for community involvement and leadership in roles deemed respectable and appropriate for their sex.

Women were particularly active in the temperance movement, one of the earliest reform movements to agitate in Wisconsin. The first temperance society west of Lake Michigan was founded in Green Bay in 1832. By the 1840s small temperance societies had formed

Rebus from the National Temperance Advocate, 1884–86. It reads: "What harm can there be in a glass of beer? None, my man, in one or two. 'Tis harmless and you're safe unless the glass of beer should get inside you."

throughout the territory. Promoters of the movement directed much of their attention toward immigrants, who often held a different view of alcohol than the primarily white Yankee proponents of temperance. Legislative attempts to stop the production and sale of alcohol only served to widen the nineteenth-century gulf between native-born Americans and recent immigrants, especially Germans, who had a long cultural history of brewing and celebrating with beer. The conflict over alcohol, which would eventually culminate in thirteen years of Prohibition beginning in 1920, represented a larger clash of cultural traditions and assimilation.

ORGANIZING AND UNIONS

During the mid- to late nineteenth century, Wisconsin also saw an explosion of organizing and organizations among working-class people. Wisconsin's first unions formed in Milwaukee—the bricklayers in 1847 and the carpenters in 1848. Because the construction of housing, docks, warehouses, and shops depended on them, the building trades were essential to the expansion of the city. Other early unions developed in trades connected to transportation, clothing, and printing. In 1867 shoemakers founded the Knights of St. Crispin, Wisconsin's first national trade union organization, which quickly grew to be the largest union in the nation.

Wisconsin's working people generally pursued a somewhat independent path within the national labor movement, pushing aggressively for state legislation rather than attempting economic actions such as strikes and boycotts. The Wisconsin movement also organized workers by industry, without regard for their particular skills. This differed from the national movement's attempts to unionize workers by skill, which often left less-skilled workers without representation. Additionally, while many national labor unions counseled political nonpartisanship, Wisconsin labor formed a close alliance with the Socialist Party and its humanitarian ideals.

The Ship Carpenters and Caulkers Association called the first successful strike in 1848, but strikes in Wisconsin would remain fairly infrequent and relatively small until later in the century. These early strikes were over issues such as low wages, the withholding of pay or irregular payment, and the hiring of unskilled labor to manage new technology. Employers used women, African Americans, and immigrants as cheap sources of labor, successfully manipulating the prejudices of white male workers. In 1863, for example, Milwaukee Typographical Union Number 23 went on strike when women were hired as compositors at the *Milwaukee Sentinel*. The strike was unsuccessful. The women kept their jobs, though at wages only slightly more than half of what their male predecessors had received.

Overall, Wisconsin workers fared comparatively well during the Civil War years, gaining leverage in industries tied to the war economy. But as the war came to an end, prices fell drastically and workers faced renewed challenges to their wages and benefits. Wisconsin workers began to form larger labor associations with national ties and more active political engagement.

As talk of reducing daily work to eight hours intensified across the nation in the 1880s, workers in Milwaukee formed the Milwaukee Labor Reform Association (later the Eight-Hour League) to agitate for the eight-hour workday. Milwaukee workers mounted extensive efforts around this issue, especially among the more militant members of the Knights of Labor under Robert Schilling. A two-year campaign to urge all employers to adopt a standard eight-hour day culminated on May 1, 1886, when all workers not yet on the system were to cease work until their employers met the demand. Eight-hour-day marches and strikes were strongest in industrial cities like Baltimore, Chicago, Cleveland, and Milwaukee. During the first five days of May, 1886, striking workers shut down all industrial plants in Milwaukee except for one: the North Chicago Railroad Rolling Mills Steel Foundry in Bay View. On May 5 a crowd of demonstrators who had sought to call out the workers still inside the huge Bay View factory was attacked by troops summoned by Governor Jeremiah Rusk. Five people were killed and four wounded. While the massacre at Bay View did not end the agitation, the violence dampened momentum for the movement and Governor Rusk became celebrated as a national hero, assumed to have saved Milwaukee from anarchy.

As the nineteenth century ended, Wisconsin labor found its political outlet in a new socialist movement built by Milwaukee's Victor Berger and, during the first decade of the twentieth century, in the support of Robert M. La Follette's Progressive movement. Factories were dangerous places for workers, and accidents killed or maimed thousands of Wisconsin citizens every year. In 1911 the first Workmens' Compensation law was passed, requiring employers to provide medical attention and compensation for loss of life and limb. After World War I, labor unions began to agitate for unemployment compensation, which finally passed in 1932, and in 1937 the Wisconsin Employment Relations Act added critical state support to the right of workers to organize.

By the early twentieth century, Wisconsinites had formed organizations, unions, and cultural institutions to meet nearly every need and to rally for or against almost every cause. In addition, towns across Wisconsin had established local or regional schools, colleges, opera houses and theaters, libraries, and clubs. In less than a century, the need for primarily economic improvements had made room for the social and moral development of the state.

7

CIVIL WAR
WISCONSIN

IN THE FIRST HALF of the nineteenth century, the economic and demographic dislocations caused by the beginnings of industrialization, immigration, and the westward movement toward low-cost frontier lands introduced new social problems and aggravated long-existing ones. The creation of new states, mostly in the west, exacerbated a particularly contentious issue that had gone unresolved since the formation of the United States: the extension of slavery. In 1861 the business of creating farms and fortunes was interrupted when national tensions erupted into full-scale civil war.

THE KANSAS-NEBRASKA ACT
AND THE NEW REPUBLICAN PARTY

By the time Abraham Lincoln's call for troops came in April of that year, Wisconsin had a critical mass of citizens who believed that slavery was wrong and secession from the Union illegal. Seven years earlier, in 1854, Wisconsinites had helped found the Republican Party, Lincoln's party, in Ripon, Wisconsin, out of anger over the Kansas-Nebraska Act. The act, introduced by Democratic senator Stephen A. Douglas of Illinois, provided for the organization of the Kansas and Nebraska territories, including the decision to allow slavery, which violated an earlier agreement. The 1820 Missouri Compromise had closed the area to slavery, but the Douglas bill, as amended, would repeal the antislavery provisions of the compromise and allow settlers to decide for themselves whether to make slavery legal. Perhaps most upsetting to Wisconsin residents, though, was the line of the bill denying noncitizen immigrants the right to vote or hold office in either territory—Wisconsin was then in the midst of rapid settlement by noncitizen European immigrants.

The Kansas-Nebraska Act provoked immediate outrage in Wisconsin. Newspapers affiliated with the Whig Party (which was divided on slavery but believed in a strong federal government that dealt with national problems) and Free Soil Party (a short-lived antislavery party), as well as a majority of the Democratic newspapers in the state, disapproved of the amendment disenfranchising aliens as well as the provision opening the territories to slavery. In the early months of 1854, anti–Kansas-Nebraska meetings were held throughout the country, including in Ripon, where under the leadership of lawyer Alvan E. Bovay, representatives of various political groups had suggested the formation of a new party—the Republican Party—to protest the bill.

In July of 1854, a convention was held in Madison to organize the new party. The members resolved "That we accept this issue [freedom versus slavery], forced upon us by the slave power, and in the defense of freedom will cooperate and be known as Republicans." Although dominated by former Whigs, members of the Wisconsin Republican Party played down their backgrounds to concentrate solely on the issue of slavery—the one issue on which they knew all Republicans could agree.

THE ABOLITIONIST MOVEMENT

Until the 1850s most Wisconsin residents had taken little interest in slavery, though a few had become ardent abolitionists. Antislavery leaders were mainly natives of New York and New England who had migrated to villages in southeastern Wisconsin. Sympathy for fugitive slaves was common in Wisconsin and grew in strength as the

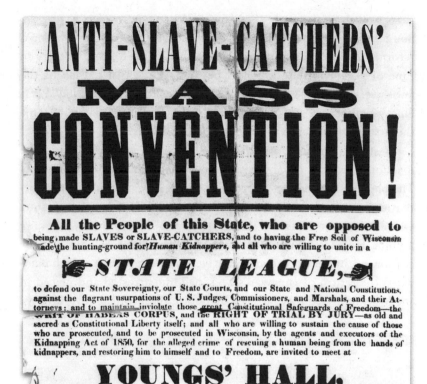

ANTI-SLAVE-CATCHERS'
MASS
CONVENTION!

All the People of this State, who are opposed to being made SLAVES or SLAVE-CATCHERS, and to having the Free Soil of Wisconsin made the hunting-ground for *Human Kidnappers*, and all who are willing to unite in a

☞ STATE LEAGUE, ☜

to defend our State Sovereignty, our State Courts, and our State and National Constitutions, against the flagrant usurpations of U. S. Judges, Commissioners, and Marshals, and their Attorneys; and to maintain inviolate those great Constitutional Safeguards of Freedom—the WRIT OF HABEAS CORPUS, and the RIGHT OF TRIAL BY JURY—as old and sacred as Constitutional Liberty itself; and all who are willing to sustain the cause of those who are prosecuted, and to be prosecuted in Wisconsin, by the agents and executors of the Kidnapping Act of 1850, for the alleged crime of rescuing a human being from the hands of kidnappers, and restoring him to himself and to Freedom, are invited to meet at

YOUNGS' HALL,
IN THIS CITY,

THURSDAY, APRIL 13th,

At 11 o'clock A. M., to counsel together ,and take such action as the exigencies of the times, and the cause of imperilled Liberty demand.

FREEMEN OF WISCONSIN! In the spirit of our Revolutionary Fathers, come up to this gathering of the Free, resolved to speak and act as men worthy of a Free Heritage. Let the plough stand still in the furrow, and the door of the workshop be closed, while you hasten to the rescue of your country. Let the Merchant forsake his Counting Room, the Lawyer his Brief, and the Minister of God his Study, and come up to discuss with us the broad principles of Liberty. Let Old Age throw aside its crutch, and Youth put on the strength of manhood, and the young men gird themselves anew for the conflict; and faith shall make us valiant in fight, and hope lead us onward to victory; "for they that be for us, are more than they that be against us." Come, then, one and all, from every town and village, come, and unite with us in the sacred cause of Liberty. *Now* is the time to strike for Freedom. *Come*, while the *free* spirit still *burns* in your bosom. *Come!* ere the fires of Liberty are extinguished on the nation's altars, and it be too late to re-kindle the dying embers.

BY ORDER OF COMMITTEE OF ARRANGEMENTS.
MILWAUKEE, April 7, 1854.

WHi Image ID 1928

Poster advertising an abolitionist convention in Milwaukee in April 1854 to prevent "having the Free Soil of Wisconsin made the hunting ground for Human Kidnappers"

years passed. By the early 1840s many Wisconsin residents were denouncing slavery as morally wrong and began organizing to discuss reform measures. They formed a Territorial Anti-Slavery Society in June of 1842; soon after, others began a Wisconsin branch of the antislavery Liberty Party, which had been founded in New York. One year later, in 1843, sixteen-year-old Caroline Quarrls became the first slave to escape to Canada through Wisconsin.

A strong uniting force in the antislavery movement was the *American Freeman*, an abolitionist newspaper based in Waukesha. The paper's third editor, Sherman Booth, had garnered national attention for his rescue and championship of the fugitive slave Joshua Glover. Glover, a Missouri slave, had fled to Racine in 1854 seeking asylum. His master, upon learning his whereabouts, came to Wisconsin and, under the federal Fugitive Slave Act of 1850, which mandated the return of runaway slaves, had him arrested and placed in the Milwaukee County Jail. Led by Booth, abolitionists from all over

WHi Image ID 39661

The "Little White Schoolhouse" in Ripon is known as the birthplace of the Republican Party.

southeastern Wisconsin surrounded the jail, broke down its doors, and helped Glover escape safely to Canada. Booth was then arrested on federal charges for violating the Fugitive Slave Act. The Wisconsin Supreme Court ultimately vindicated him, declaring the Fugitive Slave Act unconstitutional in 1855 on the basis of states' rights.

Although most Wisconsin residents disapproved of slavery, the right of black citizens to vote was another matter, disputed until after the war. In 1849 a majority of Wisconsin voters approved black suffrage, but voting rights were consistently denied to African Americans due to legal disputes over what constituted a majority. With the encouragement of Sherman Booth, Ezekiel Gillespie, a leader in Milwaukee's black community, attempted to register to vote in 1865 and was refused. Gillespie took the election inspectors to court, working with attorney Byron Paine, who had argued the Glover case a decade earlier. Gillespie's case went quickly to the Wisconsin Supreme Court, which in 1866 voted unanimously in favor of Gillespie, thus securing the right of African Americans to vote.

WISCONSIN SOLDIERS AND THE CIVIL WAR

When war broke out in 1861, Wisconsin soldiers answered the call for volunteers and enlisted. Wisconsin men and a few women (mostly in disguise) fought in every major battle of the Civil War. Governor Alexander Randall didn't simply supply the one regiment requested; rather, he organized several, each accompanied by a state agent who looked after the health and needs of the soldiers. When the war ended in 1865, 91,000 Wisconsinites had served in fifty-six regiments.

To meet the quotas required by the Civil War draft, states could pay people to serve in the place of others. Company F of the Twenty-ninth Infantry, U.S. Colored Troops, was credited to Wisconsin but was made up primarily of black Illinois soldiers who agreed to take the place of Wisconsin residents. Though most were from Illinois or Missouri, a handful of Wisconsin African Americans, such as Sergeant Alfred Weaver, a former slave from Vernon County, did join

Company F. The unit saw action mostly late in the war, in Peters-burg, Richmond, and at Appomattox, where some witnessed the sur-render of Robert E. Lee.

Recruits were trained in Milwaukee, Fond du Lac, Racine, and Madison. Camp Randall, Wisconsin's major training facility in Madi-son, also housed Confederate prisoners. Many units were composed of single ethnic groups: the Ninth, Twenty-sixth, Twenty-seventh, and Forty-fifth, for example, were mainly German, while Norwe-gians filled the ranks of the Fifteenth. The Eighth Wisconsin became known as the "Eagle Regiment" for its pet bald eagle named Old Abe, who went to battle on a perch with an American flag. According to legend, an Indian had captured Old Abe on the banks of the Flam-beau River. Until Old Abe's death in 1881, he enjoyed a wide celebrity at soldiers' reunions and fairs.

Not everyone in Wisconsin supported the war, however. Some residents were Democrats who thought states' rights should prevail, or that the nation had been taken over by Republican extremists. Others, especially German Catholics, did not support the Lincoln ad-ministration, which to them represented abolitionism, Yankee nativ-ism, and Protestant godlessness. The draft that Lincoln instituted in 1862, a particularly difficult year for the Union army, was especially intolerable to them, as many Germans had left their homeland to escape compulsory military service. On November 10, 1862, roughly three hundred rioters attacked the draft office in Port Washington and vandalized the homes of Union supporters, until troops arrived to quell the disturbance. In West Bend, the draft commissioner was beaten bloody and chased from the scene by opponents of the Civil War draft. But as the war continued and thousands of Wisconsin families lost fathers, sons, and brothers, the majority of the public came to understand the severity of the cause and the possibility of defeat. Public opinion now overwhelmingly backed Lincoln's ef-forts to preserve the union.

Wisconsin soldiers distinguished themselves in a number of bat-tles and skirmishes throughout the war. Under Cadwallader C. Washburn, the Second Wisconsin cavalry fought valiantly in many western battles, including Vicksburg. In 1864 Colonel Joseph Bailey, with the help of lumberjacks from the Twenty-third and Twenty-ninth regiments, managed to save a fleet of Union gunboats and transports stranded in the Red River of Louisiana. Using skills learned in Wisconsin's lumber camps, these men employed a technique for damming and deepening the river to aid the Union cause.

The Iron Brigade was Wisconsin's most famous war unit. Part of the Army of the Potomac, the Iron Brigade suffered unusually high casualties at Gainesville, Antietam (the war's bloodiest battle), and Gettysburg, all the while earning a reputation for unusual courage and tenacity in battle. The brigade's name came from a remark made by Union general George B. McClellan, who, seeing the men advance under murderous fire, remarked, "They must be made of iron."

Many of the Wisconsin men who fought against the South did not return. Approximately twelve thousand died, and thousands more were wounded. Wisconsin soldiers also spent time in many of the more infamous Southern military prisons, including Libby and Andersonville. These prisons were notorious for their crowding and, particularly at Andersonville, an often appalling lack of food, shelter, sanitation, and health care.

WOMEN AND THE CIVIL WAR

War created work and affected the lives of everyone, regardless of whether they joined the Union effort. Though most Wisconsin women stayed home, they literally picked up the reins that their fathers, husbands, and brothers had dropped. Women helped to keep the Wisconsin economy and their families afloat by working tirelessly in the fields. Agricultural production would have severely diminished without their labor. The Wisconsin government promised money to wives whose husbands had volunteered, but the money was slow to arrive because the priority was on funding the war effort. With the exception of some immigrants, primarily the Germans, women had rarely labored in the fields before the war. Those from New York and New England had largely tended to household duties and to outdoor work such as gathering eggs and planting a kitchen garden. Between 1860 and 1870, however, the number of women involved in industrial and commercial industries grew by over 500 percent.

Middle- and upper-class women, especially those in villages and cities, gave their time to the provision of soldiers. Setting aside their many religious, ethnic, and political differences, Wisconsin women organized to form various aid societies throughout the state. Many of these women's organizations sought to lift soldiers' spirits by sending them care packages along with news from home. The Woman's Soldiers Aid Society sent medical inspectors to improve sanitary conditions among the soldiers. They also sent thousands of dollars' worth of supplies to the front lines and to hospitals. They hired nurses for army hospitals and distributed food to soldiers. The United States Sanitary Commission was the largest volunteer organization in national history at that time.

Cordelia Harvey, widow of Wisconsin governor Louis P. Harvey, who had drowned while on a trip to bring supplies to Wisconsin troops in 1862, organized charitable activities and arranged for the transfer of many wounded soldiers to Northern hospitals. After visiting hospitals throughout the South, Harvey determined that only the cooler northern climate would restore Wisconsin soldiers to health. After repeated visits to Washington to meet with War Secretary Edwin Stanton and President Abraham Lincoln, Harvey got her way, and the Harvey United States Army General Hospital opened in Madison in 1863. Toward the end of the war, she also established an orphanage in Madison for the children of soldiers killed in service.

When the Civil War ended, Republicans, the party of Lincoln and the Union, possessed a virtual monopoly on state government. And though the Civil War ended slavery, it did not solve the complex broader issues of race and social justice in the United States and in Wisconsin.

BECOMING
AMERICA'S DAIRYLAND

WAR WAS NOT THE ONLY DISASTER to befall Wisconsin in the 1860s: chinch bugs began devouring Wisconsin wheat. This helped to launch the state, and the career of William Dempster Hoard, into a wholly different agricultural and economic direction.

WHEAT

Wheat was the earliest and most important cash crop for white settlers in Wisconsin. It required a small initial capital investment and was fairly easy to grow, allowing farmers to harvest two crops a year. The high rate of financial return made wheat an especially attractive crop for homesteaders during the middle of the nineteenth century.

From 1840 to 1880, Wisconsin was considered "America's breadbasket," producing one-sixth of the nation's wheat. The early success of wheat farming helped Wisconsin's agriculture develop more rapidly than it did in other states. Despite its appeal, wheat also had its risks and disadvantages. It was hard on the soil, which it quickly depleted of nitrogen. Depending on the vagaries of the weather and insect infestation, yield could vary substantially from year to year. By the late 1850s, the price of wheat began to drop as Wisconsin harvests and quality diminished and competition increased from farmers in Iowa, Minnesota, and further west. Infestations of tiny but voracious chinch bugs and a disease called wheat rust devastated crops during the Civil War and led many farmers to experiment with alternatives. To remain profitable, farmers had to find new, different, and more manageable crops. Feed crops, rather than cash crops, were better suited to Wisconsin's soil and climate and better suited to what emerged as the most viable alternative to wheat—dairy.

PROPONENTS OF THE DAIRY INDUSTRY

Leading the state's shift from wheat was William Dempster Hoard. Born in Stockbridge, New York, Hoard moved to Oak Grove, Wisconsin, in 1857, joining the Fourth Wisconsin Infantry during the Civil War and launching a weekly newspaper in the southern Wisconsin town of Lake Mills in 1870. Seeing the toll that low fertility and chinch bugs had taken on Wisconsin's wheat fields, Hoard remembered a similar scene in his native New York and how the dairy cow had brought respite to the depleted earth. Dairying could be the solution to Wisconsin's problem as well. Hoard began a vigorous campaign to advance dairy farming. In 1872 he organized a dairying convention in Watertown, where he helped found the Wisconsin Dairyman's Association, the first of its kind in the nation. His crusade for a prosperous dairy industry prompted his 1885 founding of *Hoard's Dairyman*, the national dairy farm magazine that is still in publication today. Hoard's success was no doubt attributable in part to the fact that many of the enterprising dairy farmers who settled in southern Wisconsin in the 1840s and 1850s were from New York. These settlers brought to Wisconsin the necessary skills for commercial dairying and butter and cheese production.

The University of Wisconsin also played a role in the burgeoning industry by actively promoting scientific research and education on dairying in the late nineteenth century. William A. Henry, the first professor of agriculture, used the university's farm to experiment with new dairying methods. The university also promoted the use of cylindrical silos for storing cattle feed during the winter and in the 1880s began offering agricultural "short courses" and "winter courses" in Madison to educate farmers on the benefits of dairying. Additionally, Farmers' Institutes, held around the state, brought farmers and scientists together to share ideas. Professor Stephen Babcock developed the first test for butterfat content in milk; the test made possible the consistent manufacture of high-quality butter and cheeses. The university's College of Agriculture pioneered testing for bacteria that led to practical methods of milk pasteurization.

Most of the state's earliest dairy operations made cheese rather than butter, even though it was harder to produce, because cheese kept longer in a time of limited and slower transportation. Charles Rockwell was one of the earliest cheesemakers, beginning production in 1837 at Koshkonong, near Fort Atkinson in Jefferson County. Anne Pickett established a cheese factory in nearby Lake Mills in 1841 using milk pooled from neighbors' cows. At first, most cheese was made on individual farms, though John J. Smith of Sheboygan County was an early exception. Smith obtained the state's first cheese vat in 1858 and became the first Wisconsin cheesemaker to market outside the state, shipping barrels of cheese to Chicago.

The transition from wheat husbandman to herdsman was difficult for many farmers, and the adjustment to the more regulated and confining routine of the factory supplier proved especially trying. In the 1870s leaders of the growing Wisconsin cheese industry organized several professional organizations to promote their product and to overcome farmer opposition to the cheese industry. Hoard's State Dairyman's Association was among the most famous of these organizations, providing marketing but also education in new dairying methods through its various publications and meetings.

New Yorkers weren't the only settlers with dairy know-how. Many German, Swiss, and Scandinavian immigrant families had experience with dairy farming in Europe and were quick to adopt dairying as a profitable way to farm in their new home. They also brought European-style cheeses with them. Swiss was among the first Old-World cheese produced in Wisconsin, originating with the state's Swiss immigrants. Italians brought mozzarella, provolone, and Gorgonzola; the French brought Camembert, Brie, and a variety of blue cheeses; the Germans, Muenster and Limburger; the English, Cheddar; and the Dutch brought Gouda and Edam. Wisconsin cheesemakers also invented new kinds of cheese: Colby, brick, and Baby Swiss. By 1915 Wisconsin had become the leading dairy state in the nation, producing more butter and cheese than any other state. Cheese continues to be a primary focus of the dairy industry, using around 90 percent of the state's total milk production.

A giant model cream separator at the Wisconsin State Fair in 1928

WHi Image ID 49793

COMMERCIAL FRUIT AND VEGETABLE PRODUCTION

Dairy wasn't the only alternative to wheat, however. Since the 1850s, agricultural reformers had urged farmers to diversify their plantings and to restore depleted soil through crop rotation and fertilization. The Civil War had encouraged experimentation and specialization with other farm products to meet wartime needs. Some of these experiments were little more than fleeting endeavors, like the Sauk County hops craze of the 1860s. Others proved more lasting.

Farmers in Waushara County, for example, established the state's cranberry industry in the central Wisconsin bogs just north of Berlin. Production soon expanded into the bogs of the central counties. Areas of southern Wisconsin also began specializing in crops. Farmers in south central Wisconsin, in Rock, Jefferson, and Dane coun-

WHi Image ID 30472

Hop pickers at the Laffan hop yard near Wisconsin Dells around 1880

ties in particular, found success with tobacco. Many other farmers turned to feed crops like corn, oats, and hay to feed the thousands of cows producing milk for Wisconsin's growing dairy industry. In 1890 Wisconsin ranked first, second, and third nationally in the production of rye, barley, and oats, respectively.

Commercial fruit and vegetable cultivation, particularly of peas, began to dominate agricultural production in certain counties in the late nineteenth century. Throughout the early twentieth century, nearly 30 percent of the state's potatoes, a basic food source for many farmers, came from Portage, Waushara, and Waupaca counties in central Wisconsin. Green peas, sweet corn, cucumbers, snap beans, lima beans, and beets all became important commercial crops in the 1880s, and Wisconsin soon led the nation in the production of vegetables for processing. And after much trial and error, apples, cherries, and strawberries emerged as viable commercial crops in a few regions of the state.

As many farmers prospered in southern Wisconsin, others, particularly newer immigrants, tried to stake claims in the northern "cutover" counties cleared by logging. The most ambitious claim for the cutover came from developer Benjamin Faast. Anyone opening a Wisconsin newspaper or agricultural journal in 1918 would probably have seen one of Faast's advertisements, reading something like this: "What a relief from the rush and turmoil, the dissatisfaction and expense of the city, to get back into the open country in a cozy little farm home surrounded by trees and flowers, fields and stock." This rural paradise, a community based on agriculture with all of the benefits and none of the chaos of urban life, was the promise Faast and his Wisconsin Colonization Company offered to those willing to take a chance on his northern dream.

Faast, a young Eau Claire land developer, had been in the land business for several years prior to the formation of the Wisconsin Colonization Company. He believed that the cutovers of northern Wisconsin could become a land populated by prosperous farmers, but first the area needed settlers. Second, those settlers needed help to achieve their dreams. To assist them, Faast offered his innovative made-to-order farm: each came with land, a house, a barn, two pigs, six chickens, tools, and seeds—everything the settler needed to get started. Faast worked with University of Wisconsin professor of landscape architecture Franz Aust to develop a complete town plan, which included a zoo, parks, a grand boulevard, and stores, all designed to take advantage of the natural beauty of the area. The largest ethnic group to settle there was Poles. Despite strong promotional efforts and state aid to help settlers remove stumps and start farming, the region did not prove conducive to agriculture and the Wisconsin Colonization Company went bankrupt in 1929.

Although farmers in the cutover region of northern Wisconsin were largely unsuccessful, agricultural production flourished throughout the rest of the state. To match the increasing scale and production levels of the state's agriculture, enterprising businessmen quickly established businesses that supplied tools and equipment to farmers. The agricultural machinery industry expanded across the southern portion of the state after the Civil War but remained strongest in the southeast, where J. I. Case, Milwaukee Harvester, and Allis-Chalmers were located.

MEATPACKING

Meatpacking also emerged as a major industry in the southeastern part of the state in the nineteenth century, directly tied to Wisconsin's growing dairy industry. Stockyards provided a market for dairy cows and baby calves destined for slaughter. The odors rising out of the stockyards of Milwaukee's Menominee River valley smelled sweet to the industrialists, bankers, and workers who made good money from the slaughtering and processing of animals in the 1850s and 1860s. Meatpacking proved a boon to the economic development of early Milwaukee, generating high profits, creating international markets, and employing large numbers of workers, many of them new immigrants.

In the 1840s the butchering and processing of livestock functioned on a small scale; farmers raised only enough cattle or hogs for local markets. Large packing houses and stockyards where farmers could send their livestock did not exist. All meat that was sold, whether beef or pork, was either fresh or heavily salted because large-scale preservation techniques did not exist. The expansion of the railroad into and across Wisconsin allowed the meat processing industry to centralize around transportation hubs like Chicago and Milwaukee. This, coupled with Milwaukee's growing population of meat-loving northern Europeans—Germans, Poles, and Norwegians—provided the impetus for small butchers to expand their operations to meet the increased demand.

Three early Milwaukee butchers—John Plankinton, John Layton, and Layton's son Frederick—capitalized on the state's agricultural resources, combining them with transportation innovations and emerging refrigeration technology to rise to the top of Milwaukee's meat industry. They encouraged the establishment of a public stockyard—a centralized terminal for livestock from around the state—to hold animals before and after sale. As more livestock entered the city, hogs and cattle running free down Milwaukee streets became an increasing problem—alleviated by the Milwaukee Stockyards, which opened in 1869. By 1880 meatpacking had become Milwaukee's leading industry.

The industry continued to grow into the twentieth century. World War I proved a bonanza, because meat packed in the United States was fed to the Allied armies in Europe. New, more innovative stockyards, located on the north bank of the Menominee River, closer to the packing plants, opened in April 1929. Trucks began to replace trains as the primary mode of livestock transport, and by the 1960s rail shipments had stopped altogether.

In the early 1970s, with the closing of the Plankinton Packing Plant, one of the last big packing plants, Milwaukee relinquished its claim to pork-packing dominance. Wisconsin's dairy industry, however, guarantees that the state's stockyards will continue to have a

WHi Image ID 2086

Women working in the casing department at the Oscar Mayer & Co. meat packing plant in Madison

role for livestock from around the state. When the wind is right, you can still catch a whiff of the stockyard's glorious past.

Today, Wisconsin agriculture is again undergoing a shift. In 1945 Wisconsin boasted more than 178,000 farms covering more than 23 million acres; that number has dropped to 76,500 farms on 15.5 million acres in 2009. The loss of farmland has not necessarily come at the price of productivity, however. The mechanization of farming has meant that farmers can produce more food on less land, using less labor. This increased productivity allowed some farms to grow bigger and bigger, while putting many smaller farms out of business. In recent years, though, small farms have made a comeback, in a sense, by supplying urban areas with specialty crops, heirlooms, and organic products—and Wisconsin has helped lead the way. Wisconsin had approximately 900 certified organic farms in

2007, second only to California. Many of them are Community Supported Agriculture (CSA) farms, where customers pay the farmer a set fee that entitles them to a share of the season's harvest. The nation's largest producer-only farmers market rings the Capitol Square in Madison each spring, summer, and fall weekend, drawing tens of thousands of people eager for sheep's, goat, and cow's milk cheeses, the zingy tang of the Green Zebra tomato, or crisp local apples. Wisconsin's new small farmers, many of them young and with little farming background, are only too happy to feed this mounting passion for seasonal food grown locally, just as it was in the state's not-too-distant past.

A woman pours water on radishes she is selling in Milwaukee.

WHi Image ID 11981

9

MANUFACTURING
THE FUTURE

MODERN SKILLED MANUFACTURING began during the Civil War
and dominated the state's economy for more than a century. While
early industry focused primarily on extracting raw materials—fur,
lumber, and lead—from the land and readying them for market,
post–Civil War manufacturing emphasized finished consumer goods
made from those materials.

As the market for consumer goods expanded, handicraft and artisan industries became less able to compete and were absorbed by a
factory system that produced standardized goods economically. Milwaukee's strong base in small, skilled craft shops provided a founda-
tion for the large manufacturing companies that came to dominate
the region. While Milwaukee was not the only city to experience
a growth in skilled manufacturing during the late nineteenth century, it had the advantages of an expanding urban market, a steady
stream of immigrant labor, and easy access to materials and customers through an ever-improving transportation system.

As the term implies, the industrial revolution did fundamentally
change people's lives, but it did not happen overnight. Mechanization and specialization changed the relationships of production; as
industrialists developed machinery to replace human labor, the con-
nections between producer and product and between producer and
consumer grew more impersonal. The textile industry was the first
to experience the effects of industrialization in the United States,

followed by agriculture, iron, steel, transportation, and communication. Famed gun maker Samuel Colt summarized the spirit of the time when he declared in 1854, "There is nothing that cannot be produced by machinery."

MACHINERY, METALWORKING, AND FOUNDRIES

Despite the state's lack of coal resources, following the Civil War Wisconsin developed a heavy industry, dependent on coal, as an adjunct to its extractive industries. Milwaukee built foundry, machinery, and metalworking businesses before the iron and steel industries were concentrated in Pittsburgh, Cleveland, and Chicago. Large-scale production of iron began when the Milwaukee Iron Company opened its doors in Bay View in 1870. The plant produced iron rails for railroads—a seemingly inexhaustible industry as railroads expanded westward—that provided a base for an enlarged foundry and machinery industry in Milwaukee.

Edward P. Allis constructed industrial machinery for manufacturers, transforming the flour-milling industry and building a worldwide reputation for his Milwaukee-based Allis Company (eventually Allis-Chalmers) in the process. In 1860 Allis purchased Milwaukee's Reliance Works and began producing steam engines and other mill equipment at the same time that many sawmills and flourmills were converting to steam power. Allis also installed a mill for the production of iron pipe to fill large orders for water systems in Milwaukee and Chicago and worked with millwright George Hinckley to develop a high-speed saw for large sawmills. By the late 1880s, the Allis Company was Milwaukee's largest industrial employer and was known the world over for its heavy machinery for mines, power plants, and public utilities. In 1901 the company merged with the Fraser and Chalmers Company, to become the Allis-Chalmers Manufacturing Company, producing machinery and other products until the late 1980s.

Cast Steel Spur Gear.
made by
The Falk Co
Milwaukee Wis
For Featherstone Foundry & Machine Co
Chicago, Ills.
Wt. 9340 lbs.
3-31-05

A factory worker poses with a steel spur gear at the Falk Corporation in Milwaukee. Falk specialized in manufacturing industrial gears.

While Milwaukee boasted the greatest variety of industries, ranging from heavy machinery to paper toys, smaller Wisconsin cities generally developed one or two primary industries, many of which did not arise until after 1900. The agricultural machinery industry was widely dispersed throughout Wisconsin by the 1870s. But as technology advanced, the agricultural industry became more dependent on foundry and machine industries, resulting in increased concentration in larger plants along Lake Michigan. In Racine, J. I. Case produced both threshers that became an industry standard and the steam engines that powered them. The many waterways of the Rock River valley supported a variety of agricultural manufacturing, particularly of machine tools, by the area's highly skilled labor force. (La Crosse, exceptionally, became a center for lumbering and riverboat building.)

After wheat moved to Minnesota and Iowa in the 1870s, large-scale papermaking took hold in the lower Fox River area, where water power was cheap and plentiful. The first wood pulp mill began operations in Appleton in 1871. Most of the paper mills on the Fox River were converted flour mills, while those on the upper Wisconsin River were more commonly associated with lumber money. Paper companies experienced their most rapid growth between 1900 and 1930, becoming the state's third largest industry by the 1940s.

Along Lake Superior and Lake Michigan, shipbuilding had been an important industry since the mid-nineteenth century and it expanded as industrial production techniques were applied in shipyards. In the 1850s construction of lake schooners began in Superior, which became an important supplier of cargo vessels during World War II. Door County's Sturgeon Bay began as a limestone and lumber shipping port but quickly became a shipbuilding center. Shipbuilding also began in the 1850s in Manitowoc on Lake Michigan. Its shipyards produced hundreds of schooners, tugboats, and steamboats in the nineteenth century, and after World War I, they began producing freighters, car ferries, oil tankers, and bulk carriers. During World War II, the Manitowoc Shipbuilding Company received a U.S. Navy contract to build submarines. The company had never built a submarine before; nevertheless, the shipyard managed to produce twenty-eight ships in the time the navy had allotted for the construction of only ten, earning the city a well-deserved reputation for its excellent shipyards.

BREWING

Another industry that took root in communities large and small was brewing. Long before Wisconsin became America's Dairyland, it was America's beer state. Brewing began in Wisconsin in the 1830s, and by the 1890s nearly every community had at least one operating brewery. Breweries were as much a part of the state's communities as churches and schools. In addition to offering steady employment to workers and buying grain from local farmers, who in turn often fed brewery by-products to their livestock, they frequently sponsored community festivals, youth groups, and sports teams. Despite beer's popularity and importance to community life, however, the brewing industry, from its beginnings, fought numerous attempts to restrict consumption and distribution of alcohol—first from temperance activists in the nineteenth century, and then, most profoundly, from national prohibition legislation in the twentieth.

Wisconsin's early brewers were drawing on a tradition of mashing, boiling, and fermenting that stretched back thousands of years. Beer came to northern Europe around 55 BCE with Julius Caesar's Roman legions. By the Middle Ages, it had become part of everyday life: the boiling and fermenting process made beer relatively free of contamination—something that couldn't always be said for the water supply. European settlers brought their beer with them to North America, and the first commercial brewery opened in New Amsterdam, now New York City, in 1612. As immigration and settlement increased and the population moved westward, breweries followed, and by the 1850s Milwaukee was contending with St. Louis for brewing supremacy.

Although Owens Brewery is generally considered the first commercial brewery in Wisconsin (opened in 1840), some evidence suggests that at least two others, one in Mineral Point and one in Elk Grove, were operating before 1840. As Owens Brewery grew, its success soon brought competition, not only in Milwaukee, but across the state. Between 1848 and 1849 twelve breweries opened in Wisconsin: Adam Sprecher in Madison, Frederick Heck in Racine, and August Fuermann in Watertown were among the most prominent brewers. By 1860 nearly two hundred breweries operated in Wisconsin, over forty in Milwaukee alone. Virtually every town had a brewery. In some cases, towns formed around breweries.

The growth of the beer industry in Milwaukee was directly related to the city's large number of German immigrants. In the 1840s Milwaukee began to take on a distinctly German character as waves of immigrants seeking economic opportunity and, in particular, religious and political freedom settled in the area. German consumers' demand for lager, a German brew, greatly expanded the city's beer industry and provided a large customer base for brewers. Many of these German immigrants were experienced brewers too, saving employers both time and money in training. The skills and experience of the German immigrants combined with Milwaukee's abundant natural resources—a good harbor, lumber for barrels, and ice for storage—to make Milwaukee a giant in the brewing industry.

THE TEMPERANCE MOVEMENT AND PROHIBITION

Despite its popularity among immigrants and the rapid growth of breweries, alcohol consumption became a controversial issue in Wisconsin. Many of Wisconsin's first white settlers came from New England—a temperance stronghold. Temperance societies formed around the state in the nineteenth century. By 1848 even Milwaukee, the center of Wisconsin brewing, had the Sons of Temperance

Grand Division. Several northern states passed prohibition laws in the 1850s, and although Wisconsin did not go that far, an 1849 law made tavern owners responsible for any costs associated with supporting drunkards. Not surprisingly, Wisconsin's German population bitterly opposed the law, arguing that it undermined individual responsibility and imposed too harsh a penalty on tavern owners. In 1851 the law was replaced with a milder statute.

Several more attempts were made to restrict alcohol production and consumption in the 1850s, but no major measures were passed again until the 1870s. In 1872 the legislature passed the Graham Law, which again made tavern owners responsible for selling liquor to known drunks. Milwaukee's city attorney challenged the law, but the Wisconsin Supreme Court held that the legislature had the right to regulate the sale of alcohol. With no luck in the courts, German Americans shifted attention to the politicians themselves, helping to defeat the Republican administration that had passed the Graham Law in 1873. The Graham Law was replaced the following year with a law that encouraged towns to work with taverns to prevent drunkenness. The new version of the law turned out to be a workable compromise for both German Americans and temperance activists, staying in effect for many years.

In Wisconsin temperance represented something far more complicated than a simple battle between those who drank and those who did not. German immigrants often remained strongly attached to their historical and cultural roots, resisting efforts at assimilation to Yankee cultural norms and frequently taking uniform stands on political and social issues such as alcohol and German-language education in schools. Moreover, saloons were increasingly seen as urban institutions and came under attack by rural people who sought to resist the problems associated with them. Temperance, therefore, became symbolic of battles between Yankees and Germans, between urban and rural residents, and between teetotaling Protestants and seemingly more broad-minded Catholics. As these forces grew in intensity, particularly during World War I, when anti-German sentiment was especially strong, and the conflict contributed to the passage of the Volstead Act in 1919.

With Prohibition, many breweries began to make "near beer," while others began to produce soda, ice cream, and cheese. Some brewers began to make malt syrup and other products that individuals could use for home brewing. But many breweries eventually had to close—some forever. In 1926 Wisconsin voters approved a referendum amending the Volstead Act that allowed the manufacture and sale of beer with 2.75 percent alcohol. In 1929 voters repealed the Severson Act, Wisconsin's prohibition enforcement law. Pledging loyalty to the "will of the people" as expressed in these referendums on alcohol, Wisconsin Senator John J. Blaine proposed a constitutional amendment for the repeal of prohibition. The U.S. Senate modified Blaine's resolution to satisfy anti-prohibitionists, allowing those areas wishing to remain dry to continue to do so, and passed the measure without delay. On December 5, 1933, the Twenty-first Amendment was ratified and national prohibition ended.

Today, brewing remains an important part of Wisconsin life, although the brewing industry has changed dramatically from its small community origins. Consolidation and commercialization has brought national, and even international, distribution for some Wisconsin breweries, while a few small brewers have survived through niche marketing and regional loyalty. In some ways, the craft brewing movement that began in the 1980s has returned brewing to its origins: the experimental brewer, the small batch, the small town.

A group of revelers celebrate as the Schlitz Engine prepares to deliver the first load of Schlitz beer since the end of Prohibition.

10

THE SPORTING LIFE

THROUGHOUT MOST OF HUMAN HISTORY, men and women have worked too hard to enjoy much leisure time. Leisure time was a privilege for the affluent or a reward for hard work rather than a right in and of itself. For most people, only the weekly Sabbath days, which already had specific purposes, broke up the incessant struggle for food, shelter, and clothing. Indeed, the Sabbath day of rest was the cause of a persistent social conflict in nineteenth- and early twentieth-century Wisconsin: Yankee Protestants often tried to impose laws regulating the conduct of Catholic immigrants, who enjoyed beer gardens, picnics, sports, and other nonreligious activities on their only day off. As industrialization mechanized work routines during the nineteenth century, many jobs became boring, requiring less mental and physical effort and providing little sense of accomplishment. People began to look for activities outside their daily work to escape boredom, develop new skills, and share experiences with family and friends. Many of the sports and games we know today were developed or became more widely known during this time.

Organized sports became popular among white settlers in Wisconsin only in the mid-nineteenth century. Until then, Americans had held assorted contests of skill but generally not in any standardized form. Pastimes inherited from Europe, such as horse racing and ball games, were particularly common, and universities increasingly became the site for organized recreation. Spectator sports with professional athletes, rules, leagues, teams, and schedules, and organizations like the National Collegiate Athletic Association, date only from the late nineteenth century. Before then, Wisconsin's different ethnic groups brought their traditional games with them and often came to dominate particular sports.

CURLING

Curling, a game in which two teams of four players slide heavy stones on ice toward a target, was one of the first games played in Wisconsin. Settlers began curling on the frozen Milwaukee River in the early 1840s and formed the Milwaukee Curling Club in 1845. Dating back to sixteenth-century Scotland, curling came to North America with Scottish immigrants and quickly spread across Canada and the northern United States, where it remains popular to this day. Mil-

WHi Image ID 7854

A women's curling team in Madison

waukee joined the Grand National Curling Club of America in 1867, playing teams primarily from the East and from Canada, although the two largest teams were in Milwaukee and Chicago. The Milwaukee curlers won their first Grand National Gordon Champion Rink Medal in 1872 and claimed the international medal in 1884. The club relocated to Riverside Park in 1915, where they remained for the next fifty-five years. Women's curling began in Milwaukee in 1949, followed soon after by mixed teams of men and women. The Milwaukee Curling Club is the oldest club in continual existence in the United States.

BOWLING

Similar in spirit to curling was another popular Wisconsin sport: bowling. The "sport that made Milwaukee famous" has been popular (and popularly associated with Wisconsin) for over one hundred years. The idea of heaving a ball at objects has existed in many variations for many centuries in many countries. English, Dutch, and German settlers all imported their own versions of the sport to North America. Nine-pin bowling was particularly popular with Germans and was the standard game in Wisconsin for many years. Although many wealthy men bowled in private clubs or on estate lanes, bowling was more closely tied to working-class immigrants, primarily Germans, and in Wisconsin took place most often in taverns. German immigrants organized teams and leagues, even encouraging women to bowl, as early as the 1880s. The popularity of bowling in taverns gave the sport a reputation for immorality, although women's involvement did help to curb some of the rowdiness, gambling, and cursing associated with all-male bowling venues.

Standardization and respectability came to bowling in 1895, when the American Bowling Congress (ABC) was formed in New York. The ABC moved to Milwaukee in 1908, further cementing the city's bowling eminence. In 2005 the ABC merged with the Women's International Bowling Congress, Young American Bowling Alliance, and USA Bowling to become the United States Bowling Congress (USBC). The USBC moved from Milwaukee to Texas in 2008.

Company-sponsored bowling teams became increasingly common in the twentieth century. The makers of Wonder Bread fielded a women's team in the 1960s that dressed in floppy chef's caps and tunics with red, blue, and yellow polka dots; in the 1930s, the team fielded by the Heil Products Company of Milwaukee included five future members of the Bowling Hall of Fame. After the repeal of Prohibition in 1933, bowling also provided breweries with a mass audience of beer drinkers. Pabst, Schlitz, Blatz, and others recruited top stars for men's and women's teams. Unfortunately, the spirit of camaraderie that surrounded bowling excluded many racial groups (as well as women) from ABC-sanctioned competitions. African Americans and women soon formed their own professional organizations to counter their exclusion from the American Bowling Congress. After World War II, labor groups challenged the organization's discriminatory rules, which were finally changed in 1950. Today, Wisconsin boasts four of the five oldest active certified centers, and has over fourteen thousand men and women's bowling leagues.

BASEBALL

Another game that emerged in the nineteenth century incorporated a bat, a ball, and bases. It was known in the United States as early as the 1820s, sometimes called "town ball" and other times "one old cat." By 1845 rules for the game were codified by the New York Knickerbockers and the game was given a name: base ball (yes, two words). Base ball came to Wisconsin with settlers from New England and New York in the mid-nineteenth century. Milwaukee enjoyed its first organized baseball game on November 30, 1859, and the following year some of the city's elite, including lawyers, bankers, and newspapermen, organized the Milwaukee Baseball Club. The Civil War ended this club, but soldiers played the game in their leisure time throughout the war.

The return of peace brought the organization of Milwaukee's Cream City Baseball Club in 1865, along with similar amateur organizations in Madison, Janesville, and Beloit. In the postwar years, the sport became more organized, and the National Association of Baseball Players counted more than two hundred clubs among its members as early as 1866. Baseball evolved from an amateur sport played by gentlemen who were unpaid to one that involved players and spectators from all classes of society, including teams whose members were paid openly or surreptitiously. The Cream City Club disbanded in 1876 but was succeeded by the West End Club, which played a mix of professional, semiprofessional, and college teams.

Baseball was also popular among Indians, besting lacrosse in popularity by 1912. Ball sports had a rich and long history among the Lake Superior Ojibwe. Unlike organized baseball, this history included women players. Reservation teams like the Odanah Braves played against teams from neighboring communities as well as semiprofessional teams from around the Midwest. Ojibwe Charles Albert "Chief" Bender, who invented the slider, became one of the most formidable pitchers in major league baseball, winning pitching honors in 1910, 1911, and 1914.

Milwaukee had a series of professional teams from 1878 through 1901, none very successful and none surviving for more than a few years. In 1901 the city became home to the American Association's Milwaukee Brewers, a minor league team that played under different owners at Borchert Park until 1952. Communities elsewhere in the state hosted clubs organized by businesses and civic organizations. Professional teams were usually minor league affiliates of the major league teams scattered around the state. Typical of these was the Wisconsin State League, made up of Class D teams in nine Fox River valley cities. Geographical closeness, local pride, and entertainment value made baseball a popular and vital part of local culture in the early twentieth century.

World War II drained manpower from the major and the minor leagues, threatening to stop play and close down major league parks.

Philip K. Wrigley, owner of the Chicago Cubs, saw women players as an answer to this difficulty and in 1943 organized the All-American Girls Professional Baseball League. Four teams from Racine and Kenosha, Wisconsin, Rockford, Illinois, and South Bend, Indiana, took to the field for the 1943 season and competed throughout the Midwest. The league eventually expanded to ten teams, including teams in Milwaukee and Minneapolis. Media and fan interest was greatest in the smaller cities, while teams in the larger cities were virtually ignored.

The women's game was modified from the major league version by shortening the distances between bases and to the outfield. Pitchers also threw underhand. The players were recruited, trained, and managed by ex–major league players or managers, and their on- and off-field dress and deportment was strictly regulated by a team chaperone and codified by handbooks and manuals. Nevertheless, in interviews, letters, and other reminiscences the players recalled enjoying their time in the league: they relished the friendships, the novelty of the experience, the travel, and the pay, which was typically about three times what women workers in traditional occupations received.

Milwaukee began seeking a major league baseball team in the 1930s, but the Great Depression and World War II defeated all efforts to locate a professional team for the city. This effort was renewed after the war, and ground was broken for Milwaukee County Stadium in 1950—before any team had made a definite commitment to move to the city. The stadium was completed in 1953, and ten thousand citizens braved icy spring weather to view it. Soon after, the Boston Braves of the National League received permission to move to Milwaukee. Twelve thousand fans greeted the arriving team at the train depot, and sixty thousand lined Wisconsin Avenue for a welcoming parade. The home opener on April 14, 1953, was a sellout, with 34,357 attending.

The Braves had several glory years, winning the World Series in 1957 and the National League title in 1958. Fans rejoiced in stars such as Warren Spahn and Hank Aaron. But team competitiveness and attendance declined, and in 1965, over strenuous objections and opposition from the city and fans, the Braves moved to Atlanta. Milwaukee County Stadium stood empty, except for occasional Green Bay Packers or Chicago White Sox games, until 1970. That year, Milwaukee businessman and baseball fan Bud Selig led the successful effort to move the Seattle Pilots to Milwaukee to become the Milwaukee Brewers of the American League. The team, now part of the National League, plays in Miller Park, a state-of-the-art stadium completed in 2001. Although the Brewers have never been the winningest team in baseball, they have enjoyed a loyal following and enthusiastic support for star players such as Hank Aaron (who played fourteen seasons with the Milwaukee Braves and two with the Brewers), Jim Colburn, Robin Yount, and Rollie Fingers. The Brewers won the American League pennant in 1982 and returned to the playoffs in 2008.

FOOTBALL

Football, like baseball, was another homegrown American sport. North American colonists had been known to kick and throw around inflated animal bladders as early as the seventeenth and eighteenth centuries. Until the 1890s, football was primarily a popular college sport. American football grew out of the popular English games of soccer and rugby, but it did not become standardized until 1922, with the establishment of the National Football League. A rival league, the American Football League, was created in 1960, and the two leagues battled for players, fans, and television contracts until they merged in 1966.

Wisconsin got a football team in 1919, when Earl "Curly" Lambeau and George Calhoun organized the Green Bay Packers after the city's Indian Packing Company agreed to sponsor a local football team. Because the company provided team jerseys and allowed the use of its athletic field, the team was identified as a company project and earned the name "Packers." The team won ten of their first eleven games against teams from Wisconsin and Michigan. Their success led Lambeau to obtain a franchise in the National Professional Football League in 1921, but financial troubles forced him to forfeit the team by the end of the year. Financial problems continued into 1922, until Lambeau, with the help of *Green Bay Press-Gazette* general manager Andrew B. Turnbull, found new backers. The "Hungry Five," as they were known, named for their hunger for a football team, regained the franchise and formed the Green Bay Football Corporation. The Packers are the only publicly owned professional sports team, a situation that makes it virtually impossible for the team ever to leave the city.

The Packers have won more league championships than any other professional football team and are the only team to win three straight titles—a feat they accomplished twice (1929–1931 and 1965–67). Lambeau was the team's star player from 1921 to 1928 and went on to coach the team for a total of thirty-one seasons. As coach, Lambeau led the Packers to championships in 1929, 1930, and 1931, and after signing future Hall of Fame receiver Don Hutson in 1935, the team won three more titles. The Packers of the 1960s, under Coach Vince Lombardi, were one of the most dominant NFL teams in history, winning five league championships in seven years. Green Bay also won the first two Super Bowls (1966 and 1967), and the Super Bowl trophy was named after Vince Lombardi in recognition of his accomplishments. The Packers returned to playoff contention in the 1990s under Coach Mike Holmgren. Holmgren's Packers won the 1997 Super Bowl but lost the chance to repeat in 1998. The Packers enjoy some of the most loyal and devoted fans of any team in the nation. Packers fans are also among the most recognizable thanks to the foam "cheesehead" hats that Ralph Bruno of Milwaukee developed in 1987 out of his mother's sofa cushion.

BASKETBALL

Professional basketball came later than some other sports in Wisconsin, arriving with the formation of the National Basketball

League (NBL) in 1937. Created by three corporations, the NBL began with thirteen previously independent teams from small Midwestern towns; these were joined by corporate teams, such as the Firestone Non-Skids. The Oshkosh All-Stars and Sheboygan Redskins were two of the NBL's top teams, with one or the other competing for the

WHi Image ID 11617

Milwaukee boys don't let the winter weather stop them from playing basketball.

league championship virtually every year. The All-Stars were back-to-back league champions in 1941 and 1942, while the Redskins claimed the title in 1943. The league lasted twelve years before merging with the Basketball Association of America in 1949, which was renamed the National Basketball Association. The Redskins joined the NBA but played only one season in the league before folding.

Professional basketball returned to Wisconsin in January of 1968, when the NBA awarded the city a franchise. The Milwaukee Bucks played their first regular season game against the Chicago Bulls in October of 1968. In 1971 the Bucks, led by Kareem Abdul-Jabbar and Oscar Robertson, won the league championship, the fastest win by an expansion team in professional sports history. The team was also notable for hiring, in 1971, general manager Wayne Embry—the first African American to serve in that position. In 1985, the Bucks were put up for sale, and fears that the team would leave Milwaukee led to their acquisition by businessman (now senator) Herb Kohl, who sought to ensure that the team remained in the city.

These and other sports and recreational activities remain a vital part of Wisconsin's social and cultural life today. From the sea of red on Badger game day in Madison to the nearly empty grocery stores on Sunday afternoons when the Packers are playing, Wisconsin residents have fully embraced the sporting life. Sports have also provided a boost to the state's economy, becoming a major industry that employs thousands of people and brings in hundreds of millions of dollars each year.

PROGRESSIVE
POLITICS

As THE NINETEENTH CENTURY drew to a close, many observers could see that the transformation of frontier Wisconsin had caused problems no one had anticipated in 1836. Large cities had spawned not only more jobs but also more poverty, disease, and crime. Businesses not only had created more efficient factories but had also trapped thousands of people at the bottom of society. The democratic institutions so painfully crafted in 1836 and 1848 had evolved into a closed system that mainly benefited party insiders. Something had to change.

ROBERT M. LA FOLLETTE
AND THE PROGRESSIVE PARTY

The genesis of political and social change reputedly occurred on September 17, 1891, when Republican Philetus Sawyer offered thirty-five-year-old attorney Robert M. La Follette a bribe to fix a court case. Furious that Sawyer would try to use money to influence the legal system, La Follette refused it, angrily denouncing the use of money to shut out the voice of the people and later saying, "Nothing else ever came into my life that exerted such a powerful influence upon me." For the rest of the decade he traveled around the state speaking out against crooked politicians, powerful lumber barons, and corrupt railroad interests. Elected governor in 1900, La Follette pledged to institute reforms. Those who followed him called themselves "Progressive" Republicans; they believed that the proper function of government was not conducting business but service to the common people.

The Progressive Republicans, led by La Follette, crafted a broad spectrum of reforms. At the time La Follette was elected, candidates for office were selected by party leaders in private caucuses. Drawing on the ideas of other reformers to make politics more democratic, La Follette successfully pushed the legislature to pass measures instituting direct primary elections, which gave voters the right to choose their own candidates for office. He supported measures that doubled the taxes on the railroads, broke up monopolies, preserved the state's forests, protected workers' rights, defended small farmers, and regulated lobbying to end patronage politics.

The Progressive movement appealed to citizens who wanted honest government and moderate economic reforms that would expand democracy and improve public morality. The techniques and ideas La Follette developed in Wisconsin made him a nationwide symbol of Progressive reform and the state an emblem of Progressive experimentation. One of those experiments was the "laboratory of democracy"—the enlistment of the University of Wisconsin's specialists in law, economics, and social and natural sciences to draft laws, provide guidance, and serve on commissions. The Wisconsin Idea, as it came to be called, held that an effective and accountable government worked best with the help of academic experts, an idea sometimes expressed as "the boundaries of the campus are the boundaries of the state." University of Wisconsin scholars John R. Commons and Edwin Witte worked closely with Progressive politicians to create programs that benefited workers, consumers, and the disadvantaged. A new Legislative Reference Library, led by Charles McCarthy, provided lawmakers with fast service from trained researchers, including a bill-drafting office that was emulated around the globe.

Elected to the U.S. Senate in 1906, La Follette brought to Washington the same kind of reforms he had promoted in Wisconsin.

WHi Image ID 2020

Robert M. La Follette campaigns in Cumberland in 1897. La Follette was elected governor in 1900.

He often spoke at length on the corruption of government and the abuse of industrial workers. Arguing that fewer than one hundred corporate leaders dominated the nation's economy, La Follette supported the growth of unions as a check on the power of large corporations. In 1909 La Follette and his wife, Belle, founded *La Follette's Weekly Magazine,* a journal that campaigned for women's suffrage, racial equality, and other progressive causes. Renamed *The Progressive* in 1929, it is still published today.

Although La Follette supported Woodrow Wilson in the 1912 presidential election, he adamantly opposed United States entry into World War I, believing that disputes between nations should be solved peacefully. La Follette also believed that America's involvement in the war would end democratic reforms at home. Critics declared him unpatriotic and asserted that his opposition to the war was political suicide; La Follette proved them wrong, and was reelected to the Senate in 1922. In 1924 La Follette ran for president on the Progressive ticket and received almost 5 million votes (most in Wisconsin), losing to Republican Calvin Coolidge, who garnered more than 15 million votes.

While La Follette was the most powerful Progressive political leader in Wisconsin, he was never able to gain complete control over the state's Republican Party or even over Wisconsin Progressives. The opening decades of the twentieth century were a time of contentious political strife and debate, and not everyone agreed about the goals and strategies of the Progressive program. Wisconsin's Progressive movement began as a small faction within the Republican Party that grew in strength by drawing support from a variety of constituencies. There were even factions within factions, each with leaders who were influential in enlisting different groups of citizens to Progressive causes. The complex program associated with Wisconsin Progressivism thus required the efforts and support of many politicians and interest groups. Although they had not initially supported the Progressive movement, Germans and organized labor later became important constituents of the movement.

La Follette's successor as governor, James Davidson, helped enact considerable progressive legislation, including laws providing for state control of corporate stock issues, an extension of the power of the railroad commission to regulate transportation, a fixing of railroad fares, and stricter regulation of insurance companies. The most important and influential progressive legislation, however, was passed during the 1911 legislative session, under Governor Francis McGovern. The 1911 legislature created the nation's first effective workers' compensation program to protect people injured on the job. It passed laws to regulate factory safety, encouraged the formation of cooperatives, established a state income tax, formed a state life insurance fund, limited working hours for women and children, and passed forest and waterpower conservation acts.

Progressivism appealed to voters who favored orderly change, rather than a fundamental shift in the economic and social order. Many of the reforms were moderate and thus acceptable to a large number of people, such as businessmen, who might not otherwise have supported the movement. Other Wisconsin citizens viewed Progressive reforms as excessive state interference, while many others wanted more sweeping changes, such as those advocated by the Socialist Party.

SEWER SOCIALISM AND VICTOR BERGER

The Socialists were particularly strong in Milwaukee. Often referred to as "sewer socialism" for its back-to-basics strategy, Milwaukee's Socialist party sought to reform the legacy of the Industrial Revolution on the local level, by cleaning up neighborhoods and factories with new sanitation systems, municipally-owned water and power systems, community parks, and improved education systems. Although Progressivism and Socialism had different leaders and spoke different languages, they were in many ways remarkably similar in practice. Socialists rejected the Progressive idea of government regulation of industry. Instead, they sought to replace the capitalist system with a planned economy of state-owned industries that would protect workers from business monopolies. Socialists believed that this change would be inevitable as the working class became increasingly oppressed by powerful businesses. Although they believed in a type of class warfare, Socialists did not advocate a violent revolution as a means of achieving their goals. Rather, Socialism was to come by ballots. Until that time came, though, Socialists supported measures to improve conditions for the working class and to achieve a more efficient administration of government—all things that Progressives wanted.

The first formal manifestation of Socialism in Milwaukee came with the establishment of the Social-Democratic Party in 1897. After the violence and chaos of the eight-hour-day campaign in 1886, Milwaukee's laboring classes had turned to political action. A Labor Party ran candidates for governor and Congress in 1886. Labor candidates continued to run for city and state offices, and the Populist, or People's Party, under the leadership of labor leader Robert Schilling, gained much of its support from Milwaukee labor in 1892 and 1894. In 1897 Milwaukee Socialists joined with Labor to form a new political party, the Social-Democrats, and Milwaukee became the first Socialist city in the United States.

Just as Robert M. La Follette came to symbolize Progressivism in Wisconsin, Victor Berger became the symbol of Milwaukee Socialism. An Austrian immigrant, Berger developed a program of political action that, while operating under the name of Socialism, was really a variety of moderate reform. Berger organized the Socialists into a highly successful political organization by drawing on Milwaukee's large German population and active labor movement.

For years, Berger published both a German newspaper and English newspaper, distributing free editions to all Milwaukee homes on the eve of elections. Milwaukee Socialists played down social theory and, like the Progressives, emphasized the need for honest government, a popular appeal in a city long notorious for corruption and administrative inefficiency. In 1910, with three parties in the running, Socialists won major electoral victories in Milwaukee. Emil Seidel became the nation's first Socialist mayor. The party also got most other city offices as well as a majority of seats on the city council and the county board. Most significantly, Victor Berger went to Washington as the first Socialist congressman.

Both Seidel and Berger lost in 1912, but by 1916 Milwaukee citizens had elected another Socialist mayor, Daniel Hoan. Although the Socialists never again completely controlled city government as they had in 1910, Hoan remained in office until 1940, and Socialists continued to exert a powerful influence in Milwaukee politics.

In 1918 Berger again won a seat in Congress, but the House of Representatives refused to permit him to take his seat, saying he had

WHi Image ID 4686

Victor Berger, left, walks arm in arm with a colleague in Milwaukee.

violated the federal Espionage Act. The previous year, Berger had supported the antiwar statement of the 1917 Socialist Convention in St. Louis, denouncing World War I as a vehicle of U.S. capitalism and imperialism. The government had also suspended mailing privileges for his English-language newspaper, the *Milwaukee Leader*. Wisconsin's governor Emanuel Philipp called a special election to fill Berger's seat in 1919, but voters again elected Berger to Congress.

However, the House still refused to seat him. Berger ran once again in 1920 but was defeated by Republican William Stafford. Although he lost the election, Berger's conviction was overturned and his mailing privileges were restored. In 1922 Berger ran for Congress and won. This time, the House allowed Berger to take his seat. He served for three successive terms.

Under Berger's leadership, Milwaukee Socialism increasingly became a program of municipal reform and good government. It also made the party a lot like the Progressives. Although their agendas were similar, Socialists and Progressives were suspicious of each other and managed to cooperate on only a few campaigns, including La Follette's 1924 presidential campaign. The Socialists wanted nothing to do with the Republican Party, the parent party of the Progressives, for they saw Republicans as weak on reform. Milwaukee Socialists and La Follette Progressives both proved by example that an honest, efficient government could work on the state and local level by introducing reforms and programs that made government more transparent and gave regular citizens more power. Socialists got support from Milwaukee voters for their citywide reform programs rather than for their allegiance to the tenets of international Socialism. Many professional people supported a Socialist mayor because he helped give Milwaukee a reputation as the best-governed city in the United States.

WOMEN'S RIGHTS

One issue on which Wisconsin was not progressive during these years was the rights of women. Women's rights had first come to the fore in Wisconsin in the 1840s at the urging of some forward-thinking early leaders who believed that women's rights should be legally protected. (Before the twentieth century, the movement called itself the woman's rights movement, a concept that embraced the idea of the individual woman as both a person and a citizen demanding rights. The plural "women" was adopted in the twentieth century to show inclusiveness.) During the 1850s, however, a flood of new immigrants, political corruption, and an economic crash dampened much of Wisconsin's utopian energy. The Civil War then largely dislodged it from the popular mind for an entire generation.

In the decades after the Civil War, the momentum for women's rights was kept alive largely through the labors of Emma Brown. Brown was the first successful female editor and publisher in Wisconsin, producing the weekly paper *Wisconsin Chief* out of her Fort Atkinson office. She had started the paper in New York in 1849, and though it became the country's longest running temperance paper, Brown also advocated for women's suffrage, exposed the harsh conditions in factories and prisons, and argued passionately for more public roles for women. From 1866 to 1889, Brown produced the weekly paper almost single-handedly.

Groups focusing on temperance and suffrage became more common in the late 1860s. The largest group to organize, the Wisconsin Women's Suffrage Association (WWSA), formed in 1869 to begin a statewide campaign. Because many suffrage activists were also leaders in the state's temperance movement, the movement generated additional hostility from the state's powerful brewing industry and from German Americans. They feared that, if given the opportunity, women would vote overwhelmingly for prohibition—a compelling reason to keep women out of the voting booths.

Women's heavy involvement in the drive to improve public schools, which seemed acceptable to many male policymakers, gave them some success with suffrage. In 1869 the state legislature passed a law allowing women to run for school boards and other elective school offices. In the 1870s neighboring states began allowing women to vote in elections related to school and temperance issues. Following their success in gaining the right to run for local school boards, the WWSA began an all-out suffrage campaign in the legislature in 1884. The legislature refused to consider full suffrage but gave women the right to vote in any election "pertaining to school matters." Many suffrage leaders feared that if school board candidates appeared on a general ballot alongside other offices (rather than on a separate school ballot), women would not be allowed to vote at all—a fear that was confirmed in the spring elections of 1887.

In many parts of the state that spring, women's ballots were accepted without question, but in Racine, the ballot of WWSA leader Olympia Brown was rejected. Casting her vote for municipal offices on the basis that they too affected local schools, Brown sued to force local officials to accept her ballot. Circuit Judge John Winslow agreed with Brown, but the state Supreme Court reversed the decision in *Brown v. Phillips* (1888), contending that doing so would give women the right to vote for all offices, which was not what the legislature had originally intended. The court also held that women could not use ballots that included any offices other than school offices, since there was no way to verify that women had only voted for school offices on a system of secret ballots. Candidates for school office would have to be listed on a separate ballot—something the legislature refused to allow local governments to do. This effectively nullified the school suffrage law of 1869.

The suffrage movement changed tenor in the 1890s. While the first wave of the suffrage movement had advocated radical rather than gradual change, a new generation of suffrage activists began to work for incremental reforms. Led by Theodora Winton Youmans of Waukesha and Ada James of Richland Center, women's rights advocates began relying heavily on women's clubs to promote suffrage as just one part of a broader platform of civic reforms. The WWSA soon gave way to the Wisconsin Federation of Women's Clubs (WFWC) as the leader in the campaign for women's rights.

These new reformers concentrated on two short-term goals: placing more women in influential positions of state government and making the school suffrage law actually work. In 1901 the legislature finally authorized separate school ballots, enabling women to vote for school offices. La Follette, whose wife Belle was an attorney active in the women's movement, advanced the first goal by appointing women to state boards and commissions. He also helped

*Theodora Youmans, president of the Wisconsin Women's Suffrage Association,
holding a Wisconsin flag*

pass laws that ensured that women would always have positions on some state boards.

But the same Progressive leaders who endorsed worker and consumer rights were reluctant to grant women's suffrage because they knew that their male supporters opposed it. On November 4, 1912, Wisconsin men voted against suffrage by a two-to-one margin. When politicians blocked new suffrage referenda in 1913 and 1915, Wisconsin women threw their energy into the national cause. A suffrage amendment to the U.S. Constitution finally passed in 1919, and the Wisconsin Legislature became the first to ratify it on June 10, 1919, giving women the right to vote in federal elections. The right to vote in state elections did not come until 1934, however, when the Wisconsin constitution was finally amended. Wisconsin did pass the nation's first equal rights bill in 1921, granting women full equality with men under civil law. Unfortunately, the generalities of the law and its subjection to court interpretation rendered the law essentially meaningless for women.

ALTHOUGH IN SOME WAYS INCOMPLETE, spotty, and occurring in fits and starts, the Progressive movement was notable for the dedication of politicians and citizens to improvement, expansion, growth, and change, and for their firm belief in their ability to make the world a better place for everyone. The Progressives continued as a movement inside the Republican Party until 1934, when La Follette's sons, Governor Philip F. La Follette and Senator Robert M. La Follette Jr., created a short-lived third party, the Wisconsin Progressive Party. The party disbanded in 1946, due in part to social change wrought by the Depression and World War II, marking the end of the La Follette era in Wisconsin.

12

WORLD WAR I

WORLD WAR I INTERRUPTED the Progressive era and strained Wisconsin's democratic traditions. The same Progressive-oriented people who had believed that change was possible became fearful and suspicious during wartime. What designated something or someone as "American" became particularly narrow, and anyone who spoke with an accent or voiced dissent became suspect.

In 1917 Americans—Wisconsinites, in particular—were sharply divided over participation in the war. The strict neutrality that had characterized U.S. foreign policy up to that point shifted now toward involvement on the side of Great Britain, largely due to Germany's decision to resume unrestricted submarine warfare. The U.S. officially entered the war on April 6, 1917. Nine of Wisconsin's eleven congressmen, including Wisconsin's most famous politician, Senator Robert M. La Follette, voted against the declaration of war. This was a hazardous course and a source of deep distress to the many Wisconsin citizens who passionately embraced the war effort as a patriotic call to arms.

Wisconsin's antiwar sentiment came from many sources. The politically dominant Progressive and Socialist parties generally opposed American entry, as did the state's German American population. Though his opposition risked his reputation and influence, La Follette's position was straightforward, never straying from President Woodrow Wilson's declared policy of strict neutrality from

1914. La Follette maintained that nothing in the aims and arguments of the belligerents on either side could possibly concern Americans or their interests enough to justify their participation.

Milwaukee Socialists were another voice for antiwar sentiment in Wisconsin. European Socialists had exhibited a startling shift around this time: ignoring their own previous professions of international solidarity, most supported the aims of their national governments. Nevertheless, American socialists continued to call for an international Socialist movement and adopted a militant antiwar position two days after Congress declared war. Milwaukee Socialist Victor Berger, an outspoken opponent of war and militarism since the 1890s, voted for the antiwar plank and ardently defended his position. Despite this, Berger ultimately viewed American participation in the war as a potential boon to the Socialist cause, because he thought the military's demand for food, shelter, and munitions would force the government to adopt some socialist ideas.

As one of the largest immigrant groups in Wisconsin, German Americans were deeply affected by the war. Despite the wide spectrum of political and religious beliefs across Wisconsin's German American community, the vast majority maintained a strong cultural unity based on pride in German accomplishments, a vigorous German-language press, and a persistent conflict with the dominant Yankee cultural values. This tension centered largely on the issue of alcohol. Protestant Yankees generally favored temperance, while brewing and beer drinking were accepted norms in German culture. As a consequence, many German organizations devoted to preserving German heritage and defending civil liberties were subsidized by the brewing and distilling interests, which further inhibited German American efforts to win sympathy outside their community.

A HYSTERICAL CONFORMITY

The declaration of war unleashed a particularly virulent form of hysterical conformity among the American people. Many Wisconsin citizens were acutely sensitive to charges of disloyalty due to the publicity surrounding La Follette's criticisms, the antiwar influence of the Socialist party in Milwaukee, and the large number of people with German ancestry. During 1917 and 1918, German culture became suspect. Some Wisconsin towns refused to teach German in their schools and German-language books were burned in Wisconsin streets. Indeed, anyone with a German name was a target for harassment; a widely publicized notice from the American Defense Society stated that a German American, "unless known by years of association to be absolutely loyal, should be treated as a potential spy." In April 1918 in Ashland, Northland College professor E. A. Schimler was kidnapped from his boarding house by a masked mob, tarred and feathered, and made to walk back home. His crime? Having a German name and teaching the German language to students.

Despite many sources of outspoken opposition to the war, the majority of Wisconsin citizens did support the war and did so with a more measured response. Business, labor, and farmers all enjoyed great prosperity at the time, and, aiming to safeguard these gains, more than 118,000 citizens entered into military service. Wisconsin was the first state to report in the four national draft registrations and was highly commended by federal authorities for its efficiency. The Wisconsin National Guardsmen in the Red Arrow Division gained a reputation for their fearless and effective fighting. In all, 1,800 Wisconsin citizens died in the war.

WARTIME SACRIFICE

Wisconsin was also the first state to organize both state- and county-level Councils of Defense, which helped to educate citizens on the war and the sacrifices it demanded of them. As part of an agricultural state, Wisconsin's State Council of Defense was particularly interested in solving the national food crisis that developed in 1917 with the country's entry into the war. Three years of war had decimated European food supplies and the Allies had come to depend on the United States for food. Now with the United States planning to send hundreds of thousands of men into the field, each requiring huge quantities of food, something had to be done. Council chairman Magnus Swenson of Madison began vigorously promoting food conservation through the cultivation of home gardens and the institution of meatless and wheatless days. Swenson's policies became so admired that Herbert Hoover adopted many of them as

WHi Image ID 33439

Many women joined the workforce at the Four Wheel Drive Company in Clintonville to build trucks for the army. They helped the company manufacture more than 20,000 trucks during the war.

WHi Image ID 102£1

Rodney Williams from Delafield shot down five enemy aircraft in July 1918, earning him the honorary military distinction of "ace."

head of the newly formed federal Food Administration. Even the Socialist mayor of Milwaukee participated in preparedness parades, cooperated with the draft, and established a Milwaukee council of defense at the same time that he defended the rights of opposition voices like Victor Berger.

When the war ended in November 1918, Wisconsin citizens returned to the Progressive leadership of La Follette and his followers. In the Senate, La Follette opposed the Versailles Treaty and American membership in the League of Nations, seeing the treaty as a violation of Wilson's pledges to remain neutral and the League as an organization for victors only. The United States never joined the League of Nations.

World War I had ended, but another even more severe calamity was coming. Spread in part by the interaction of soldiers from many countries, a global flu pandemic marked the end of the war. Known variously as the Spanish Flu or La Grippe, influenza killed an estimated 50 million people worldwide, nearly 700,000 in the United States—far more than were killed in the battlefields during four years of World War I. The first cases in southern Wisconsin were reported in September 1918. By December influenza had sickened almost 103,000 residents and killed more than 8,000. The State Board of Health declared that the flu epidemic, even more than the war to end all wars, would "forever be remembered as the most disastrous calamity that has ever been visited upon the people of Wisconsin."

13

CHANGING HABITS
OF CONSUMPTION

APPLETON, WISCONSIN, is far from the laboratory in Menlo Park, New Jersey, where Thomas Edison perfected the incandescent bulb and other uses for electric power. Yet it was in this Fox River city in 1882 that the first plant to commercially generate electricity was lighting homes and factories. Only nine years earlier, in 1873, Reverend Dr. J. W. Carhart of Racine had designed and driven a steam-powered, self-propelled vehicle—one of the first automobiles in the United States. By 1910 Wisconsin produced nearly as many automobiles as Detroit.

These two innovations in everyday life had nearly as much impact on Wisconsin life as the political, military, and economic events of the early twentieth century. Electric power and automobiles helped to reorient American life and values, changing patterns (and hours) of work, the location of homes, and modes of transportation. Wisconsin was a national leader in both technologies.

ELECTRICITY

On September 30, 1882, history was made with the glow from a carbonized bamboo filament inside a small bulb at the home of Henry J. Rogers on 625 West Prospect Avenue in Appleton. Rogers, executive of the Appleton Paper and Pulp Company, had become interested in the idea of electric light after a fishing trip with a Western Edison

Electric Company salesman. With the installation of an Edison Type "K" dynamo electric generator and using the water power of the Fox River, Rogers's plant began to transmit power to local paper mills, the water company, and some of the city's wealthiest families. Other generating plants soon followed, finding an eager market in communities seeking to replace manufactured coal gas as a source of light.

Electricity could also provide power for small appliances, like irons and vacuum cleaners. In 1916 the Milwaukee Electric Railway and Light Company published the pamphlet "The Electrical House that Jack Built," written in verse as a parody of the well-known nursery rhyme, to show how electric appliances could transform home life. Illustrated with drawings that resembled children's books of the period, it celebrated the convenience, comfort, and health enjoyed by users of electrical appliances:

> *This is the porch where in the breeze*
> *My lady irons at her ease*
> *When the summer makes the kitchen hot—*
> *The Iron stays warm, the ironer not.*
> *Fatigue's to her a stranger quite,*
> *She does her work and finds it light—*
> *In the Electrical House that Jack Built.*

In the early twentieth century Wisconsin developed a significant small electric appliance industry, which included the Hamilton Beach Manufacturing Company of Racine. Hamilton Beach developed the first practical electric drink mixer in 1911 at the urging of William Horlick, who wanted to make it easier for consumers to mix up his powdered "malted milk." The company is still around today, relocated to North Carolina.

The availability of electric power for urban transportation, elevators, and factory machines transformed cities across the United States. Electric railroads made suburban living possible for people of all classes, and the central city often became the center of business

A man shows off an incandescent lamp switchboard at the nation's first commercial electric light plant in Appleton in 1882.

while employees rode streetcars from residential neighborhoods. Investors began promoting interurban trolleys as a way to connect adjacent cities, characterizing automobiles as toys for the wealthy. A former manager of Milwaukee's street railways, John I. Beggs, had become Wisconsin's utility tycoon by 1901, managing light, traction, and gas companies in the Milwaukee and Fox River valley area. Beggs envisioned an interurban system running from Chicago to Green Bay, with branches stretching to Madison and Janesville. Unfortunately for investors like Beggs, automobiles soon won out over light rail.

When engineers harnessed the power of Niagara Falls in 1896, Wisconsin investors and utilities began to look seriously at the state's many rivers as possible sites for hydroelectric power stations. The high costs associated with hydroelectric power, however, dampened the enthusiasm of many early entrepreneurs. Though Wisconsin had more than four hundred dams by 1935, steam continued to supply the vast majority of the state's power. Cost also discouraged the formation of small power companies, leading, inevitably, to its control by three giant corporations. The regulation of utilities by the Wisconsin Railroad Commission brought relatively economical electrical power to urban markets, but rural areas were largely ignored. As late as 1930, only one in six farms had electrical service.

As the financial squeeze of the Depression affected the entire nation, a growing urban and suburban population demanded more efficient food production from the nation's farmers—an efficiency that many believed could be gained through rural electrification. Many farm leaders and members of Congress believed that farmers needed electrical service under conditions and prices that would allow for its full and productive use. Waiting for commercial electric companies to provide services, however, was too expensive and inefficient. In 1935 President Franklin D. Roosevelt established the Rural Electrification Administration (REA) to help farmers meet the growing need for power. Although, like many New Deal programs, the REA began as a program of unemployment relief, it soon became primarily a lending and investment agency. The government began to encourage and grant preference to nonprofit, cooperative organizations of farmers in order to develop their electrical transmission infrastructure.

The task of organizing rural electric cooperatives was generally left to local leaders; they organized meetings, collected fees, enrolled consumers, and worked with the REA on program details. The REA provided farmers with low-interest loans to help them build their own lines and provide their own electricity. On May 7, 1937, Wisconsin's first cooperative, Richland Electric Cooperative, went into service. Within fifteen years, 90 percent of American farms had electricity.

While rural electrification efforts began primarily to assist farmers, electric power also contributed to the growth of the tourist industry in northern Wisconsin. Resort owners realized that electricity would make the area more attractive to tourists, so the Bayfield cooperative established a special summer rate for these resorts. With affordable electricity, the tourist industry boomed in both summer and winter.

AUTOMOBILES

The real boon to Wisconsin's tourism industry, though, was automobiles, which became a common sight on state roads at the turn of the twentieth century. In 1875, two years after Reverend Dr. J. W. Carhart designed his self-propelled, steam-powered vehicle, the Wisconsin legislature offered a $10,000 prize to the winner of a race between Green Bay and Madison in an effort to find a "cheap and practical substitute" for horses. Two groups of inventors took up the challenge and the race was run in 1878 between two steam-powered automobiles named for the cities in which they were invented: the *Oshkosh* and the *Green Bay*. The *Oshkosh* won, traveling an average of six miles per hour to Madison; the *Green Bay* didn't make it at all and was shipped back home.

By 1899 gas-powered automobiles began to appear more regularly in the state. Driving provided a new experience for Wisconsin citizens. It also provided a boost to the state's economy, as Wisconsin developed into a regional center for the automobile industry.

Edward Joel Pennington was one of the first Wisconsin manufacturers to produce automobiles. In 1895 he joined Thomas Kane and Company in Racine to build the "Kane-Pennington Hot Air Engine." Unfortunately, the company soon failed. Bicycle manufacturer Thomas B. Jeffery proved a far more successful businessman, building what became one of Wisconsin's most profitable automobile companies. Trained in England as a maker of scientific instruments, Jeffery came to Chicago, where he built bicycles called "Ramblers," experimenting with automobiles on the side. In 1900 he sold his business and moved to Kenosha, where, in 1902, he produced fifteen hundred new Ramblers, borrowing the bicycle name for his automobiles. Anticipating Henry Ford, Jeffery sought to provide quality automobiles for the average American family. The Jeffery family sold the business in 1916 to Charles W. Nash, who quickly made the Kenosha plant the largest producer of automobiles outside Detroit.

In 1917 Kenosha's Rambler plant began producing the Nash. Additional plants were soon built in Racine and Milwaukee, and Nash negotiated a contract with the U.S. Army that made the Nash Motor Company one of the largest producers of trucks in the nation.

Bicycles also played an important part in the development of Harley-Davidson in Milwaukee. William Harley and the Davidson brothers (William, Walter, and Arthur) designed a motorized bicycle with a two-cylinder engine that became the company trademark. During World War I, they produced eighteen thousand motorcycles for the military to use for dispatch work.

Other Wisconsin companies joined the race to produce automobiles before World War I. In Racine, successful wagon maker Mitchell-Lewis began building cars in addition to wagons. By 1911 the Mitchell-Lewis Motor Company had become the city's largest employer, employing two thousand workers to build the company's fashionable touring cars. The company was later bought by another Wisconsin automaker, the Nash Motor Company, in 1925.

In Hartford, hardware dealer Louis Kissel moved into automobile production in 1906, producing one of Wisconsin's most prized custom automobiles. The Kissel Kar attained international renown for its classic design and outstanding performance. During World War I the Kissel firm began to produce trucks for the army, employing as many as fourteen hundred workers. The company suffered severe financial losses during the Depression, however, and ended production of the famous Kissel Kar in 1930.

William Besserdich and Otto Zachow of Clintonville invented the four-wheel drive in 1908. Their Four Wheel Drive Company helped make Clintonville a center of heavy truck production. During World War I, the company reached an international market, producing 14,473 trucks for the U.S. government.

WHi Image ID 32354

An interior view of the truck assembly room at the Winther Motor and Truck Company in Kenosha

ROAD IMPROVEMENTS

Despite the number of automobiles being produced in the early years of the twentieth century, the development and maintenance of Wisconsin roads remained a low priority for government officials. Trains remained the most popular mode of transportation, and funding went to create additional rail lines instead of toward road improvements. The Good Roads Movement of the 1890s and early 1900s sought to transform the road conditions, but mainly to help farmers rather than drivers. The poor condition of Wisconsin's roads made it difficult for farmers to maneuver their wagons to market, and Good Roads promoters campaigned for state-financed road improvements. After the State Aid Road Law passed in 1911, roads began to be paved with gravel. By 1916 the State Highway Commission, recognizing the needs of the automobile, began to establish a system of highways throughout the state.

Improved roads also helped towns attract tourists, particularly in northern Wisconsin. A 1922 highway census revealed that more than three thousand automobiles had passed through Rhinelander from other regions. That fall, businessmen organized the Northern Wisconsin Resort Association to encourage tourists to come to the area and to improve the services available to them. By 1923 over two thousand members from various businesses had joined, and the organization changed its name to the "Wisconsin Land o' Lakes Association" to better represent the broad range of services its members offered. The association established tourist bureaus in Chicago and Milwaukee, estimating that advertising would reach at least two million people a week. They even dared to believe that tourists might find their experience so enjoyable that they would settle permanently in northern Wisconsin—an effort that proved somewhat successful, though primarily in the area of vacation homes. Other parts of the state endowed with great natural beauty—the Apostle Islands and Chequamegon Bay on Lake Superior, Door County in the northeast, and Lake Geneva in the southeast—experienced similar growth as summer vacation destinations for motoring tourists.

TOURISM

With increasing numbers of people traveling by car, new patterns of vacation behavior began to develop. Vacationers who took the train expected to find a resort or hotel waiting for them. Freed from the strictures of railroad schedules and stops, tourists began to set up camp along the sides of the road, creating a new nuisance for farmers and communities left with the refuse of a previous night's stay. To combat the problem without discouraging people from coming, communities began to provide free campgrounds with ovens as well as community houses with bathrooms. The better the campground, though, the more likely tourists were to overstay their welcome, incurring considerable municipal expense. Most cities began charging fees by the late 1920s, and soon private campgrounds overtook municipal sites in both number and range of services.

One of the most popular vacation travel routes was Highway 13, which ran from the Illinois border near Beloit to Ashland and the Bayfield Peninsula. Resort owners called the highway "Lucky 13" and promised tourists that they could find anything they wanted along its path. Brochures and pamphlets were sent out to encourage travel along the highway, highlighting various sites in each of the towns. In 1941 the federal government published *Wisconsin: A Guide to the Badger State*, which promoted the fun and excitement of driving along Highway 13.

Tourism continues to be a major industry, especially in northern Wisconsin. Nearly every weekend, the roads to northern Wisconsin towns—Minocqua, Hurley, Hayward, Bayfield—or just simply to "the lake" are filled with cars. Some pull powerboats, snowmobiles, or trailers; others are loaded with canoes, kayaks, bicycles, tents, or cross-country skis. Tourists also go to Wisconsin Dells in the south-central portion of the state to enjoy the natural beauty and water parks that have made the area one of the top vacation destinations in the Midwest.

The increasing availability of consumer products and new technology changed the way people lived, worked, and vacationed in the twentieth century, a trend that continues to this day. All of this consumption has not come without its price, however. While tourism has certainly bolstered the state's economy, the construction of vacation homes and resorts along with other outdoor activities have also threatened animal habitats and led to deforestation and polluted lakes and streams. And the electrical appliances that make our lives easier have also found their way into our state's landfills. Making consumption and travel habits sustainable for future generations is the challenge that faces residents today.

14

DEPRESSION

THE AUTOMOBILE, ELECTRIC APPLIANCES, and other new technologies expanded business opportunities in the 1920s. To fuel that growth, many companies borrowed money from banks. Factory production and stock prices rose as more and more people bought new goods and a share in the profits being made from them. The horrors of World War I behind them, many felt optimistic about the new possibilities opening for women and small entrepreneurs and believed that the prosperity of the decade would continue indefinitely.

The stock market crash came as a surprise and drastically curtailed a creative period of economic growth throughout the country. On October 29, 1929, many more investors tried to sell stock than tried to buy new shares. Stock prices tumbled far below what investors had paid. Within hours people who owned great wealth on paper were unable to pay back their loans. Many tried to sell stock to raise cash, which further lowered prices; in only ninety days the stock market lost 40 percent of its value and $26 billion of wealth disappeared.

In Wisconsin, people turned from sneaking bootleg beer into jazz halls to devising ways to survive the worst economic depression in the nation's history. Wisconsin suffered severely as factories closed, wages dropped, and unemployment swelled. Although farmers were somewhat more secure than factory workers in terms of food and shelter, they still suffered a dramatic decline in income and property values.

Stories of the Depression's effect on Wisconsin residents survive in numerous letters, diaries, and recollections. The recollections of one woman, Edna Veale of Kenosha, exemplified a common experience. Three months after her marriage in 1929, Veale's husband lost his job. Fortunately, Veale had a job at the grocery store that earned her $16 a week, but even so, they were forced to move in with her father, four brothers, and a sister for several years to make ends meet.

Milwaukee was hit especially hard by the Depression, despite the city's diversified industries. Between 1929 and 1933, the number of people who had jobs in the city fell by 75 percent, and Milwaukee County provided some form of direct relief to 20 percent of the population. Milwaukee's mayor, Daniel Hoan, organized a national conference of mayors in 1933 to pressure the federal government for help. Adding insult to injury, a severe drought settled onto the Midwest in the early 1930s, crippling Wisconsin agriculture.

STRIKES AND SOCIAL CONFLICT

Policymakers' efforts to overcome the economic stagnation took place in an atmosphere of intense social conflict. Extremists from across the political spectrum thought they understood who was to blame for the current catastrophe and what should be done to fix it. Certain in their own viewpoints and anxious about the future, many activists felt justified in using force to try to bring about their ends.

Violence broke out in several rural counties over milk prices. Wisconsin was the country's largest producer of milk at the time, but low prices had forced many farms into foreclosure and caused widespread rural poverty. Thousands of farmers banded together in 1933, working mainly through the Wisconsin Farm Holiday Association and the more radical Wisconsin Cooperative Milk Pool, in an attempt to raise prices by withholding milk from the market. Not all farmers supported these efforts, however, and their resistance was met with intimidation and violence. Strikers constructed roadblocks to prevent milk deliveries and to force trucks to turn back.

Strikers also forcibly dumped milk at the roadside—some thirty-four thousand pounds in Racine in one instance—tainted delivered milk with kerosene, and, in a few cases, threw bombs at creameries. In response, the state called out the National Guard, which responded with violence of its own. At least three farmers were killed in clashes with picketers, protesters, and soldiers. Disturbing as they were, however, the milk strikes were too localized to influence dairy prices nationally, and the strikes petered out in November of 1933. The market for milk gradually improved, though not before Wisconsin farmers lost an estimated $10 million during the strikes.

In Milwaukee, the number of strikes increased sevenfold between 1933 and 1934. Industrial workers, faced with falling wages and rising lay-offs, organized more tightly as labor leaders sought to increase union influence. This trend was helped by the passage in 1931 of Wisconsin's first comprehensive labor code, which gave all workers the right to organize and sanctioned a range of union organizing activities.

Even with strengthening protections for workers that helped protect their wages and jobs, a major stumbling block to recovery was the failure of financial institutions. Despite a trend in the 1920s toward consolidation, the state still had many small banks in 1929, and when the stock market crashed, large numbers of them closed their doors forever. The situation became so precarious that in March 1933, Governor Albert George Schmedeman declared a two-week statewide banking moratorium to settle the volatile atmosphere. This collapse of Wisconsin's banking system was unmatched in state history and recovery was slow and painful. Banking in Wisconsin would not exceed its pre-1929 strength until 1942, when military production for World War II had begun to lift the country's entire economy.

RELIEF PROGRAMS

Even before Roosevelt's New Deal started to bring federal relief in the mid-1930s, the Wisconsin legislature enacted relief programs of its own. Under the leadership of Robert M. La Follette's sons, Senator Robert M. La Follette Jr. and Governor Philip F. La Follette, Wisconsin Progressives tried to develop programs—known as Wisconsin's "Little New Deal"—to respond to the needs of struggling people. Many of the La Follettes' ideas would be echoed or expanded on the federal level in the New Deal. The legislature also passed the nation's first unemployment compensation law. At the time, University of Wisconsin economist John R. Commons had been promoting unemployment compensation for two decades, but during the prosperous 1920s the bill he wrote was repeatedly introduced without success. As more and more people lost their jobs after the 1929 crash, however, public opinion changed and a new unemployment bill, drafted by Harold Groves, finally passed in early 1932 and became a model for the nation.

Seeing its success, President Franklin D. Roosevelt appointed University of Wisconsin economists and Wisconsin natives Arthur Altmeyer and Edwin Witte to serve on the Committee on Economic Security in 1934. After studying the unemployment and pension programs of other nations, Witte and Altmeyer devised a program that established a national retirement-age insurance system, federal-state unemployment insurance, and aid to dependent mothers and others who could not work. With the passage of the Social Security Act in 1935, the federal government extended protection to the unemployed, the aged, and the disabled.

Also in 1935 Roosevelt authorized the Works Progress Administration (WPA) to put unemployed Americans to work on public projects. More than 8.5 million Americans built bridges, roads, buildings, airports, and parks for an average monthly salary of forty-one dollars. The WPA didn't just create manual labor jobs; it also created jobs for white-collar workers and for those in the performing and fine arts. Particularly novel were the special projects like the Federal Writers' Project, which hired writers and researchers to prepare state and regional guidebooks, organize archives, and conduct historical and sociological investigations. The Federal Theatre Project sent

WHi Image ID 54580

Women from Milwaukee County repair clothing for families as part of the Milwaukee Sewing Project, which was similar to the Milwaukee Handicraft Project.

scores of stock companies out to tour the country, bringing drama to communities where it had been known only through the radio. The Federal Arts Project gave unemployed artists the opportunity to decorate hundreds of post offices, schools, and other public buildings with murals, canvases, and sculptures. Musicians organized symphony orchestras and community singing. A subsidiary project, the Milwaukee Handicraft Project, put unskilled women to work making curtains, furniture, toys, rugs, dolls, and costumes under the enthusiastic leadership of art professor Elsa Ulbricht. Unlike most other WPA projects, the Handicraft Project willingly hired African Americans, creating a demand for positions so great that two shifts had to be created to keep up.

Another work relief program, the Civilian Conservation Corps (CCC), designed to reduce unemployment among young men, focused on the conservation of natural resources on local, state, and federal lands. From 1933 through 1942, the CCC assigned nearly 165,000 men to 128 camps throughout Wisconsin, planting trees, building roads, fighting fires, and stocking streams. The federal CCC program was segregated by race and, against the objections of both Senator La Follette and Governor La Follette, Wisconsin's black volunteers were sent to black camps in Illinois. In Wisconsin, 92,000 men carried out conservation projects such as tree planting, trail building, and erosion control in 45 camps around the state. Today, many of the foot bridges, beaches, and hiking trails in Wisconsin state parks survive as testimony to the effectiveness of these federal and state programs.

While early relief efforts succeeded in helping many urban workers, New Deal programs for farmers were largely ineffective. The Agricultural Adjustment Act (AAA) tried to raise prices by asking farmers to destroy crops, thereby reducing supply while demand remained stable. It identified nine basic crops and paid farmers to decrease their acreage of them. While this program helped some large farms, small farmers and those who grew crops outside the chosen nine saw little benefit. The AAA limitations on milk production provided a slight improvement in dairy prices, but it was far from a permanent solution for Wisconsin's struggling dairy farmers. Low market prices and drought made the decade of the 1930s a desperate time for most Wisconsin farm families.

Roosevelt's success on the national level helped to temporarily discredit the Republican Party and led Wisconsin Progressives, particularly the La Follettes, to organize a separate Progressive Party in 1934. They called for an improved conservation program, the distribution of milk as a public utility, the initiative and referendum on the national level, and a popular referendum on war—the last, a vestige of Progressive opposition to the World War I. Both La Follettes campaigned under the slogan "Run with the La Follettes and win"—and win they did.

When the votes were counted, the Progressives controlled the state legislature and sent seven men to Congress.

But it was not to last. Governor La Follette's attempt to launch a national Progressive Party in 1938 ended in failure with his defeat to Republican Julius P. Heil, who systematically demolished the state agencies created under La Follette's "Little New Deal." Senator La Follette disbanded the Progressive Party in 1946, rejoining the Republicans, and tried without success to keep the Senate seat he had held since his father's death in 1925. The demise of the Progressive Party and the defeat of both La Follettes marked the end of the La Follette era in Wisconsin.

Unemployed men stand in line for Civil Works Administration jobs in Madison in 1933.

WHi Image ID 16987

Although New Deal policies and programs had done much to reduce the suffering of Wisconsin's residents, it was America's entrance into World War II that finally stimulated the economy. This time, there was little opposition to war. Nazi victories and the threat of fascism justified U.S. participation to nearly all Wisconsin residents. Wartime industries provided jobs for Wisconsin's urban workers, while farmers increased production to meet the demand of feeding soldiers and civilians, helping to create a wave of economic prosperity in the 1940s.

15

WORLD WAR II

THE OUTBREAK OF THE SECOND WORLD WAR ushered in a period of great affluence and unity in Wisconsin. The Depression years receded into the background as defense spending and military preparedness resulted in defense contracts for Wisconsin businesses. Rather than the dismal unemployment that had plagued the 1930s, labor was in high demand and wages and prices rose accordingly.

A NEW PROSPERITY

Both industry and agriculture shared in this prosperity. Wisconsin citizens quickly shifted to wartime production, becoming more dependent on orders from the military than ever before. Manitowoc, Sturgeon Bay, and Superior once again became centers of shipbuilding. The Badger Ordnance Company quickly grew into one of the largest manufacturers of ammunition in the world. Farmers, who had intentionally slowed their production only a few years earlier, now supplied large quantities of dairy products, vegetables, eggs, and meat to the military and civilian populations. State businesses received orders worth $4.6 billion during the war. Industrial employment provided one of the most valuable ways for civilians to aid the war effort, yet the men who normally would have worked in these factories were needed on the battlefield. Wisconsin women replaced many of the men who had joined the armed forces.

The demands of war opened doors that women's rights advocates had been unable to budge. "Without the great reservoir of woman-power ready to help, American manpower might not be enough to do the job," proclaimed a 1942 Allis-Chalmers Manufacturing Company pamphlet. "So—Jane, Dorothy, and Mary are donning coveralls. They are pinning up their hair, and getting dirt on their hands. And they like it . . . Yes—our girls, Uncle Sam's nieces, are doing their share to help win the war." Before the war, Allis-Chalmers had employed only 144 women (about 3 percent of the total workforce), but by December 1941 the number had increased to 750. At the end of the war, nearly 25 percent of the factory's entire workforce was comprised of women.

Women who worked in factories encountered many problems never faced by the men they replaced. Some women, for example, had children who needed childcare. Women were also paid far less than male workers with the same or even less experience. And while wartime necessity may have upended some traditional gender con-

Women workers at Moe Brothers metal shop in Fort Atkinson

ventions, it didn't happen in every job, nor for all women, and certainly not permanently.

Antiwar sentiment virtually ended with the United States' entry into the war. There was no crusading antiwar enthusiasm or strong opposition minority. Although Senator Robert M. La Follette Jr. and then-Governor Philip F. La Follette had opposed American involvement in the war, upholding the legacy of their father, both conceded in the end that the threat of fascism in the face of Nazi triumphs justified U.S. participation and muted their criticisms of the war effort.

In October 1940 Governor Julius Heil established a state council of defense to coordinate with the federal and local defense programs. The University of Wisconsin and other colleges introduced military training classes for students and shared facilities with branches of the armed services. Many Wisconsin men received basic training at Camp McCoy, while Madison's airport (now named Truax Field) was an important center for radio communication training. Additionally, the United States Armed Forces Institute, in cooperation with the University's extension service, offered college correspondence courses to servicemen throughout the world.

WISCONSIN'S SOLDIERS

Roughly 320,000 Wisconsin soldiers served in the armed forces during the war. All told, more than 8,000 Wisconsin soldiers died and another 13,000 were wounded in combat. The majority of Wisconsin soldiers were draftees who served in units comprised of men from around the country. Wisconsin's National Guard formed a substantial part of the new Red Arrow Division, which helped to maintain the respected reputation of its predecessor from World War I by remaining undefeated in the Pacific theater. When they were deactivated in January 1946, the Red Arrow Division had been in service for more than five years—longer than any other American army. Eleven of its members won the Congressional Medal of Honor and another 3,000 earned medals for valor and service. These honors came at a high price: more than 11,000 men received Purple Hearts (awarded in the name of the president to those who have been wounded or killed) and 3,000 Red Arrows died.

Richard Bong, born and raised on a farm near Poplar, Wisconsin, left for the U.S. Army Corps a volunteer flying cadet in 1941 and came home one of the most decorated heroes of the war. Bong joked to his mother in a 1942 letter written on the eve of his departure for Australia that with the way things were going in the war, he wouldn't "see home until the war is over or unless I get over there and become a hero so they send me home for a couple months. I guess that's what I'll have to do." And that's what he did. In his first air battle, Bong shot down two enemy planes. By the time his tour was over, Bong had downed forty enemy planes and won twenty-six decorations for his service. General Douglas MacArthur personally awarded him the Congressional Medal of Honor in 1944. Heroism had its downside, however, as the army was reluctant to endanger the life of America's flying ace by sending him into combat. In December 1944 Bong was ordered back to the United States. He died at the age of twenty-four while testing a new jet aircraft in California in 1945.

WOMEN IN THE MILITARY

Men were not the only ones called to the battlefield. Approximately 9,000 Wisconsin women also served in the military. While most were involved in healthcare, many also served as parachute riggers, cryptographers, weather observers, and ferry pilots. Each branch of the military had specific units for women. Women served in the U.S. Navy as WAVES (Women Accepted for Volunteer Emergency Service), in the Coast Guard as SPARS (Semper Paratus–Always Ready), in the Army as WACs (Women's Army Corps), and in a special reserve force in the Marine Corps. Female pilots, or WASPs (Women Airforce Service Pilots), brought new aircraft from the factory to airfields. Ellen Ainsworth, a twenty-four-year-old nurse from Glenwood City, was the only woman from Wisconsin killed in action during the war.

WHi Image ID 11365

Milwaukee photographer Dickey Chapelle took this photo of Red Cross worker Betty Sullivan serving coffee at Kobler Field in Saipan to a B-29 flight crew.

CIVILIAN SACRIFICES

While many Wisconsinites left for service, most citizens actively participated in the war effort at home. Until the war ended in August of 1945, the daily challenges of wartime shortages of food, gasoline, and other essential goods were a part of everyone's life. Gasoline rationing began in 1942. Most drivers received four gallons a week, later reduced to two. The government also instituted a national speed limit of thirty-five miles per hour to help conserve gas and rubber tires. Wisconsin's Consumer Interests Committee organized county consumer councils and organizations to educate people on basic cost- and product-saving measures. Citizens were urged to plant gardens, carpool, preserve food, and learn some general home maintenance. Classes in home and car repair were organized especially for women. As the development of strategic bombing led to new forms of civilian defense, citizens also participated in air raid drills and blackouts.

But for many people the hardest wartime adjustment was likely the meat ration. Brats, roasts, steaks, and assorted fish and fowl were staples in Wisconsin, where hearty meals fueled hard physical labor. By 1942 the meat ration was two and a half pounds per person per week. Black markets for meat and other rationed goods soon sprang up. Although the number of people who traded black market meat was unknown, the government believed that the practice was common enough to warrant the issuing of booklets warning about the dangers of underground meat. Most people, though, accepted rationing as a necessary sacrifice.

While people on the home front rationed food, Wisconsin agriculture expanded tremendously to meet the wartime food needs of the Allies. Milk, meat, eggs, and canned vegetables, all of which Wisconsin was well positioned to supply, were in great demand. Farmers benefited from unusually good weather and used technology, including commercial fertilizers and hybrid corn, plus increasingly mechanized barn and field operations, to achieve record levels of production. Milk production, in particular, expanded by 20 percent between 1939 and 1943.

At the same time that war enlarged Wisconsin's industrial and agricultural resources and capacity, increasing production and employment levels also raised the standard of living and the state's economic security. Once the war ended on September 2, 1945, people in Wisconsin, as everywhere, wanted to put the war behind them. But the war had changed the social and economic fabric of the state and country. There would be no return to the past for veterans, workers, women, farmers, villagers, and city dwellers. In particular, a vocal anti-Communist movement led by Wisconsin Senator Joseph McCarthy would undermine the state's Progressive and Socialist traditions and dramatically alter Wisconsin's postwar culture.

International Harvester poster promoting "victory gardens" and war bonds, 1943

16

CULTURE of FEAR

AFTER WORLD WAR II, FOREIGN AFFAIRS played an increasingly important role in the lives of American citizens. The United States and its allies competed with the United Soviet Socialist Republics (USSR) and its allies for political and economic dominance around the world. Known as the cold war, this rivalry between the United States and the Soviet Union shaped almost every aspect of international politics, as well as many domestic concerns, until the fall of the Berlin Wall in 1989 and the dissolution of the USSR in the early 1990s.

In the late 1940s people in Wisconsin were divided over issues such as the creation of the United Nations, support for European recovery, and the growing power of the Soviet Union. But when postwar Europe divided into Communist and capitalist camps and China's Communist revolution succeeded in 1949, public opinion generally shifted toward supporting the protection of democracy and capitalism against Communist expansion. That tension came to a head in Korea.

THE KOREAN WAR

Overshadowed by World War II, the Korean War has often been called America's "forgotten war," though, like Vietnam, it was part of a larger cold war struggle to extinguish Communism. In 1950 North Korean troops invaded South Korea, which was an American ally. Seeking to protect South Korea and to prevent the spread of Communism in Asia, President Harry Truman sent General Douglas MacArthur to command the United Nations forces. Lasting three years (1950–53), the Korean conflict was dominated by politically motivated negotiations and stalemates that delayed the armistice and cost thousands of lives.

Around 132,000 Wisconsin citizens served in Korea. Some, like Dale King, who recalled his experiences years later to the D. C. Everest Area School District Oral History Project, were among the 111 Wisconsinites taken prisoner during the war. Captured by the Chinese on April 25, 1951, King spent two years, four months, and four days inside a POW camp, doing hard labor and suffering interrogations, starvation, and poor health. He was lucky to survive. Nearly 35 percent of POWs died in the camps.

The Korean War also marked the first time in American history that military units were officially racially integrated. Mitchell Red Cloud, a Native American from Hatfield, was one of five men from Wisconsin to receive a Congressional Medal of Honor for his service in Korea. Women were also involved, serving in the Mobile Army Surgical Hospitals (MASH) as well as other divisions of the military.

When hostilities ceased with the signing of the armistice on July 27, 1953, Chinese armies remained on their side of the North Korean border. The North and South, separated by a wide demilitarized zone along the 38th parallel, entered a long period of tense relations that continues to this day. Korea, besides being the first armed confrontation of the cold war, also created the idea of a "limited war," where two superpowers fight their battles in another country and where the objective is not the total destruction of the enemy. Korea also expanded the cold war, which had, to that point, been mostly confined to Europe.

Because Communism led, in practice, to tight restrictions on personal freedom and government ownership of business, it threatened American ideals of individual liberty and free enterprise. Communist expansion in Eastern Europe and Korea fueled Americans' anxiety that their way of life was under attack. This anxiety launched the career of Wisconsin senator Joseph McCarthy.

SENATOR JOSEPH McCARTHY

After several uneventful years in the Senate, McCarthy made headlines when he announced in a February 9, 1950, speech in Wheeling, West Virginia, that he knew of 205 Communists currently working in the State Department (he later reduced this number to fifty-seven). This wasn't the first time McCarthy had raised the specter of Communism—in a 1946 campaign, back before Communism was a major national issue, he had accused his Democratic opponent of being a "little megaphone" for the Communists. But in 1950, as American men and women were preparing to sacrifice their lives in combat against a Communist enemy in Korea, this speech garnered great publicity. Capitalizing on people's fears of encroaching Communism, McCarthy launched a public campaign aimed at eliminating the supposed Communist infiltration of government and foreign policy. His pronouncements catapulted him to national prominence and provided a strong platform for his reelection.

Easily reelected in 1952 and chosen chair of a Senate Permanent Investigations Subcommittee, McCarthy took it upon himself to expose Communists and their sympathizers—not only in government but throughout all of American political and cultural life. Under his leadership, the Subcommittee interrogated more than five hundred people. McCarthy's accusations were often unsubstantiated, but in a political and cultural climate filled with fear, they gave him considerable power. Hiding behind the veil of national security, McCarthy and his staff often refused to reveal their sources of information at a time when simply being called before his committee could ruin an individual's career. Fearful of being named Communist sympathizers themselves, many leaders of labor unions and professional organizations joined in the Red Scare hysteria of the early 1950s. Some intellectuals and activists did refuse to answer his questions or appear before his committee despite the threat to their personal well being. Several famous Hollywood producers and scriptwriters were among the best-known citizens blacklisted by their employers for refusing to cooperate with the committee. But it was McCarthy's accusation in 1953 that the military was harboring Communists that ultimately led to his downfall. TV commentator Edward R. Murrow helped to expose McCarthy's tactics during an investigation on his program and publicly denounced his actions as a threat to Americans' core democratic values. In December 1954 the Senate officially rebuked McCarthy for "conduct unbecoming a senator."

During the brief period he was in power, McCarthy attained worldwide recognition, symbolizing the frenetic anti-Communism that gripped American foreign policy in the 1950s. Virtually unknown outside Wisconsin in 1950, McCarthy was politically destroyed by 1955. He died in 1957. During those five years, though, McCarthy was

WHi Image ID 3614

Senator McCarthy, middle, during the Army-McCarthy hearings

a hero and champion to those who believed the country had lost its authority in the postwar years, and an evil, dangerous man to those who believed he exploited fears and violated standards of honesty.

ATOM BOMBS AND NUCLEAR WAR

Communist fear also drove Americans underground and under desks in the 1950s. After the first atomic bomb was dropped on Japan in 1945, Americans realized a new era was upon them, one in which humans had the ability to destroy the world. Fear of nuclear warfare and the adverse effects of atomic radiation pervaded popular film, literature, and other forms of mass culture. Once the Soviets detonated their first atomic bomb in 1949, apprehension escalated. Many Americans now believed that an atomic war was on the horizon and that they would be among the victims.

With tensions running high, the American Legion, a leader in anti-Communist sentiment, decided to stage a "Day Under Communism" in 1950 to educate Americans about the pending threat. Mosinee, Wisconsin, a small paper mill town, was chosen for the event. Joseph Jack Kornfeder, a former Communist who had been trained in Moscow's Lenin School in "methods of political warfare," helped bring an aura of believability to the spectacle, which included the printing of a pink-hued edition of the *Mosinee Times* newspaper, praising the virtues of Joseph Stalin.

Nationally, the federal government created the Federal Civil Defense Administration (later called the Office of Civil Defense) to instruct the public on how to prepare for a nuclear assault. Families received educational materials and teachers taught children atomic attack survival techniques at school, including the famous "duck and cover" maneuver. Children were also sold identification bracelets so their bodies could be identified in the debris. While none of these methods would likely save anyone in the event of a nuclear attack, the government did help calm fears by giving people concrete actions to take to make them feel safe.

The most common form of recommended protection was a fallout shelter. Most survival manuals assured people that two weeks after an attack, they could emerge from their shelters and eventually return to their normal lives. Infrastructures, such as water mains, roads, and electrical wires, were expected to remain undamaged or be easily repairable. The government began to build public shelters staffed with trained volunteers and stocked with civil defense equipment and supplies.

Worried that nearby Chicago would be the target of an atomic bomb, Paul and Edith Sobel, like many Wisconsin residents, decided to construct a fallout shelter in their Racine home. They later donated virtually the entire contents of their shelter to the Wisconsin Historical Society. The Sobels sent away for all the literature the local Civil Defense Office could provide, chose one of the suggested plans, and built the shelter into their basement. The result was a ten-by-eight-foot room meant to house a family of five for two weeks. It included an eighteen-inch-thick cement ceiling, walls of solid concrete block painted a cheerful color, and a second wall, or baffle, outside the door to supposedly protect the occupants from radiation. The Sobels stocked their shelter with supplies recommended in government pamphlets.

While Americans were bombarded with fearful images of atomic annihilation, they also saw the atom portrayed in positive and humorous ways. America's growing interest in all things atomic prompted manufacturers and other commercial businesses to use the atom symbol and the word "atomic" to capture public attention and to project images of progress and modernity. "Atomic," "nuclear," and "H-bomb" became slang terms used to signify things that were awesome or monumental. Americans also began laughing at some of their own atomic fears in movies and comic books, including *The Atomic Kid* (1954), starring Mickey Rooney as a man with special powers gained from an atomic blast, and *Ma and Pa Kettle Back on the Farm* (1951), where Pa discovers that he can run electrical appliances after he puts on some radioactive overalls.

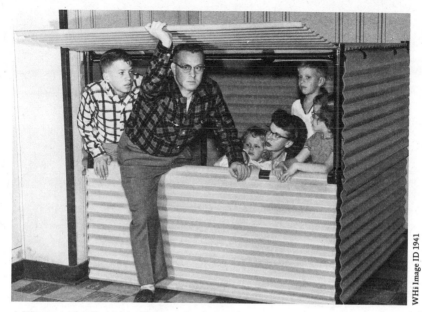

A Wisconsin family inside their new bomb shelter in 1952

WHi Image ID 1941

Fear was an easily exploitable commodity in the postwar years, and it drove much of the nation's social, cultural, economic, and political activity of the period. By the mid-1960s, however, new events and concerns drove the alarm over nuclear war from the minds of many Americans. The Cuban missile crisis of October 1962, a confrontation between the United States and the Soviet Union over Soviet missile installations in Cuba, represented the peak of anxiety about nuclear war, but afterward the Soviet Union and the United States agreed to take the first steps toward nuclear disarmament. At the same time, increased interest in the space race, which had started with the Soviet launching of the Sputnik satellite on October 4, 1957, made images of space exploration the new symbols of modern technology. While progress toward disarmament allowed many Americans to breathe a sigh of relief, other concerns, such as the civil rights movement and the escalating Vietnam War, now occupied center stage.

17

MIGRATION AND CIVIL RIGHTS

WHEN ROSA PARKS REFUSED to give up her seat on the bus on December 1, 1955, leading first to a bus boycott in Montgomery, Alabama, and later to sit-ins, marches, and demonstrations elsewhere in the South, many Wisconsinites viewed the civil rights movement as a "southern problem." But as the movement spread northward in the 1960s, Wisconsin was forced to confront its own brand of racial inequities—Wisconsin's segregation was imposed by historical custom and popular prejudice rather than by the force of law and statute.

AFRICAN AMERICANS IN WISCONSIN

African Americans have lived in Wisconsin since well before statehood, but for a long time their numbers remained small—less than three thousand in 1910, for example. Almost all lived in cities and faced very limited employment opportunities, since most factories were segregated until the start of World War II. Job opportunities during World War I attracted some African Americans to the Milwaukee area, but by 1930 the black population had increased by only seven thousand. Wisconsin, unlike its neighboring states of Illinois and Michigan, did not experience sizable interwar migration from the South, primarily due to the nature of the state economy. Wisconsin's agricultural and skilled manufacturing jobs did not offer many opportunities for African Americans, who had historically been relegated to unskilled fields due to discriminatory practices. Most farms were owner operated and had relatively little demand for hired labor. Likewise, the skills required for much of the state's industry, coupled with the fact that the unskilled jobs were already taken by earlier immigrants, prevented most African Americans from finding jobs. Other factors also played a role in discouraging black settlement, including local covenants regarding housing and scarcely concealed prejudice in many communities. Additionally, the overall small number of African Americans did not provide a base of family support or general assistance to attract new migrants.

African Americans were especially hard-hit by the Depression. As late as March of 1940, 46 percent of Wisconsin's black population was unemployed, compared to 13 percent of whites. Finding themselves in largely unskilled jobs, African Americans in these positions were the first to go when businesses were in trouble.

Between 1940 and 1960, Wisconsin's African American population increased by nearly 600 percent, from 12,158 in 1940 to 74,546 in 1960. Many were veterans who'd lived outside the segregated South for the first time during the war. Drawn to jobs in industrial cities during World War II, a number of African Americans stayed to raise their families. Wisconsin's African American population remained extraordinarily concentrated in a few urban areas, with nearly 90 percent living in Milwaukee, Beloit, Madison, Racine, and Kenosha. Yet even in these cities, it was possible for most white people to have little contact with African Americans due to restrictive racial covenants and local custom. Seven Wisconsin counties did not have a single black inhabitant in 1960, while another thirty-two had fewer than ten.

Most of the new migrants came from Mississippi, Arkansas, and Tennessee. For many, Milwaukee represented one in a series of stops that began in the South and moved northward. Black institutions, like the Milwaukee Urban League, served as vital links for new arrivals to learn about housing and jobs, particularly in industrial fields. The continuing demand for labor brought on by the manufacturing boom during the war and the efforts of the Milwaukee Urban League opened an abundance of industrial jobs during and after World War II and brought more and more southern black migrants to Milwaukee in the 1940s and 1950s. The job opportunities were largely confined to black men, however. Black women could not often obtain the same skilled, unionized, and high-paying jobs as black men.

Manufacturing jobs not only provided employment, but also brought upward mobility that allowed many blacks to join Milwaukee's property-owning middle class. But while the war temporarily improved the economic state of African Americans, these gains were not matched in reduced housing segregation or alleviation in other forms of discrimination. Racial discrimination and segregation ran rife, especially in Milwaukee, where the ties of ethnicity and religion had long resulted in highly segregated residential patterns. Even among the city's European immigrant groups, these patterns were generations old and not easily surmounted.

African Americans in Wisconsin had been struggling for their civil rights for more than a century before the movement began to attract national headlines in the 1960s. In 1866, Milwaukee's Ezekiel Gillespie successfully sued for the right to vote, and in the 1930s, William Kelley of the Milwaukee Urban League began to fight for the rights of black teachers to work in the public schools. These early efforts were especially difficult because the state had so few African Americans before the middle of the twentieth century.

However, as more African Americans came to Wisconsin seeking jobs in urban areas, race became the overriding factor in determining where they were allowed to settle and how they could become a part of Wisconsin society. And as they encountered segregation in housing, employment, and education, African Americans began to organize in greater numbers to remedy these injustices.

The civil rights movement of the 1950s and 1960s was one of the most dynamic periods of social interaction and change in US history. Since the end of the Civil War, African Americans had struggled for the full recognition of rights accorded to them in the thirteenth (abolishing slavery), fourteenth (equal protection), and fifteenth (voting rights) amendments to the Constitution. Frustrated by the lack of practical effect brought by constitutional amendments and by legal redress in the mid-twentieth century, African Americans increasingly rejected gradualist, legalistic approaches. As the primary tool to bring about desegregation, these legal efforts faced continued resistance by proponents of racial segregation and voter suppression.

THE CIVIL RIGHTS MOVEMENT IN MILWAUKEE

At the time, Milwaukee was one of the most segregated cities in the nation. By the 1960s African Americans accounted for 15 percent of the city's population. Most lived in the "Inner Core," a near-north neighborhood that had become a site of increasing volatility due to limited job opportunities, poverty, and segregation. This kind of frustration generated urban violence and inner-city riots across the nation in cities such as Los Angeles and Detroit. On July 30, 1967, riots broke out in Milwaukee after police attempted to stop fights at a downtown entertainment spot. In response, Mayor Henry Maier declared a state of emergency and asked the governor to call out the National Guard. Eight days later, four people were dead and more than fifteen hundred had been arrested.

Efforts at reforming segregation in Milwaukee focused on segregated housing and schools. In August 1967 after five years of inaction by city officials, the NAACP Youth Council marched to Kosciuszko Park (in a predominantly white neighborhood) to protest the Common Council's refusal to pass an open housing ordinance. Alderperson Vel Phillips, Milwaukee's first female and first African American alder, had first introduced open housing legislation in March 1962 and continued to submit it to the council for approval, despite its being repeatedly voted down. The August 1967 march expressed the frustration of the black community but also drew the wrath of three to five thousand white residents, who shouted obscenities and threw objects at the marchers. They particularly focused on the march's leader, a white Catholic priest named Father James Groppi. Groppi was an important figure in the civil rights movement, playing an instrumental role in drawing attention to Milwaukee's segregation through his frequent demonstrations and arrests. Daily demonstrations continued throughout the winter of 1967–68.

WHi Image ID 48149

Father James Groppi stands with Vel Phillips on the hood of a bus before a crowd of Milwaukee NAACP Youth Council activists.

RESIDENTIAL AND EDUCATIONAL SEGREGATION

In April of 1968 the federal open housing law passed, preventing racial discrimination in 80 percent of the nation (20 percent was exempted on various technical terms). That same month, the Milwaukee Common Council approved a desegregation law even stronger than the federal one that exempted only owner-occupied buildings with no more than two units. Adoption of this ordinance ended the more militant phase of the civil rights movement in Milwaukee, though loopholes in federal and city housing policies allowed segregation to continue. Housing patterns in Milwaukee, as in other cities, were shaped by real estate agents, city zoning laws, and banking institutions that refused to lend money to African Americans moving into white neighborhoods. Suburbanization also contributed to segregated housing, as whites increasingly moved out of Milwaukee and left the inner city to African Americans—a trend that persists to this day.

Residential segregation had inevitably produced school segregation as well. Despite the 1954 decision in *Brown v. Board of Education* of Topeka, Kansas, which declared racial segregation unconstitutional, school segregation remained widespread, often because of segregation in the city's neighborhoods. In a 1960 survey of schools, the NAACP found that schools in Milwaukee's central city were 90 percent black. On August 28, 1963, the Congress of Racial Equality (CORE) in Milwaukee organized the first civil rights demonstration in the city. A year later, in May 1964, they organized a boycott of predominantly black schools that drew the participation of more than half of the African American students.

In 1965 Lloyd Barbee pledged to make the courts do what the school board would not and filed a lawsuit that challenged segregation in the Milwaukee public schools, the first of its kind in the nation. Barbee, a civil rights advocate and state legislator, founded the Milwaukee United School Integration Committee (MUSIC), which became the primary vehicle for his efforts to desegregate schools. The case *Amos, et al. v. Board of School Directors of the City of Milwaukee*, filed on behalf of thirty-two African American and nine white students, charged that the board practiced and allowed discrimination in the public schools. Barbee demanded that Milwaukee end the illegal but real segregation of its schools. He argued that the Milwaukee School Board had drawn district boundaries based on segregated housing patterns and other discriminatory policies, citing as evidence that most of the schools outside the city's Inner Core had less than 10 percent African American students.

More than a decade later, on January 19, 1976, Federal Judge John Reynolds ruled that Milwaukee schools were illegally segregated and ordered the school board to take immediate steps to integrate the schools. The board appealed the decision to the U.S. Supreme Court, which ordered a new trial. Finally, in March of 1979, the case was settled and the school board agreed to implement a five-year desegregation plan that, though not perfect, began to address some significant schooling issues.

Segregation and discriminatory practices in Madison, though perhaps less publicized, were no less common than in Milwaukee. While many white residents were proud that blacks were not discriminated against in restaurants, public transportation, hotels, schools, or hospitals, African Americans still faced inferior situations in both employment and housing. Unlike Milwaukee, Racine, Beloit, and Kenosha, Madison did not have the industrial manufacturing sector to hire unskilled and semiskilled workers, and many employers were reluctant to provide on-the-job training. While few businesses openly admitted to discriminatory hiring policies, these practices persisted throughout the 1960s and 1970s. Moreover, as in Milwaukee, poor housing and residential segregation led African Americans to campaign for open housing laws in Madison.

In the 1970s the nation's attention shifted from the black civil rights movement to other issues, such as Vietnam and the environment, and to other social groups that had begun to assert their rights. Inspired by the civil rights movement and demands for equal protection, the gay rights movement began campaigning against discrimination in jobs and housing. The 1969 Stonewall riots in New York helped to transform the movement from small, localized activism into a widespread protest for equal rights and acceptance.

In 1982 Wisconsin became the first state to outlaw discrimination on the basis of sexual orientation. And in 1998 Tammy Baldwin of Madison became the first woman and first openly gay nonincumbent to be elected to the U.S. House of Representatives. More than 150 Wisconsin companies offer domestic partner benefits, extending benefits, particularly health insurance, available to heterosexual employees to gay and lesbian couples and unmarried heterosexual couples. Despite these notable firsts in gay rights, however, in 2006 Wisconsin voters approved an amendment to the state constitution that defined marriage as between one man and one woman, prohibiting marriage for gay and lesbian couples.

18

VIETNAM

As the antiwar movement and American involvement in Vietnam escalated in the mid-1960s, civil rights activism merged and changed. Many of the students leading the war protests had gotten their first taste of activism earlier in the decade, helping southern blacks with desegregation and voter registration. They now turned their attention and energy to stopping what became the longest and costliest war in U.S. history.

More than fifty-eight thousand Americans died and more than three hundred thousand were wounded in a war fought primarily in Vietnam from 1959 to 1975. The United States entered the war incrementally from 1950 until 1965, when President Lyndon Johnson began aggressively bombing North Vietnam and sent U.S. Marines to defend South Vietnam. The United States became involved in the war for a number of reasons, many of which evolved over time but largely had to do with containing Communism. Increased U.S. involvement was matched by a rise of antiwar protest in the 1960s, as dissenting groups formed at many of the nation's universities, including the campuses of the University of Wisconsin. In the early 1960s, however, the majority of Americans supported the Johnson administration's claim that it was fighting to stop Communism in Southeast Asia—as the country had in Korea a decade before—and were unaware that this gradually escalating war would forever alter American society.

The war pitted the North Vietnamese and the National Liberation Front (NLF, or Vietcong) against the United States and the South Vietnamese army. From 1946 until 1954, a unified Vietnamese population had fought for their independence from France. At the end of that struggle, the country had been temporarily divided into two governing units. North Vietnam, allied with the Soviet Union and China, was governed by Vietnamese Communists who sought to unify Vietnam under a Communist government like that in China. South Vietnam, on the other hand, many of whose leaders had collaborated with the French, was allied with the United States and sought to create a democratic capitalist society.

As the two governments continually fought against each other after 1954, the United States began to supply more and more aid and soldiers to South Vietnam. In 1965, when it appeared the North might win, the U.S. sent large numbers of troops to prevent the South from collapsing. By 1969 more than five hundred thousand U.S. soldiers were stationed in Vietnam and another 1.2 million were positioned elsewhere in Southeast Asia. Although Congress never officially declared war, the conflict in Vietnam took the lives of many soldiers and brought social, political, and economic costs.

More than 57,000 Wisconsin residents served in Southeast Asia; 1,239 did not return. American soldiers were, on average, younger than those who had served in World War II, nineteen as compared to twenty-six. They also came from disproportionately rural and urban working-class backgrounds. Because the army had a policy of rotating servicemen into Vietnam for a year at a time, soldiers returned home individually rather than as members of a military unit, undermining the cohesiveness among veterans found in previous wars.

ANTIWAR SENTIMENT

Opinion of the war was as mixed among those who fought as it was at home. Soldier Benjamin Morgan, in an April 1969 letter to University of Wisconsin–Madison history professor Edward Coffman, wrote, "This is a war begun strictly by political elements in the American Congress. The authorization they receive [sic] to act under the Gulf of Tonkin resolution was artificially expanded to pronounce a mandate of military measures . . . Vietnam has not been worth the price. War has never been productive, and our investment here will reap very little return." Veterans who felt similarly had organized the Madison Veterans for Peace in Vietnam in 1967. They sought to challenge the notion that dissent indicated a lack of patriotism, particularly among former soldiers. Others were more enthusiastic, or at least more willing to trust the motives of the American government.

At home, many Americans at first supported the Vietnam War, but as the Johnson administration increased U.S. involvement, dissatisfaction turned into organized protest. Early protests coalesced around questions about the morality of U.S. military involvement. Antiwar sentiment increased following the Tet Offensive of 1968

WHi Image ID 54991

Anti-Vietnam War protestors demonstrate outside the Badger Army Ammunition Plant in Baraboo.

and after Johnson's successor, President Richard M. Nixon, escalated U.S. involvement. Protests also grew rapidly after the 1970 invasion of Cambodia and the 1972 Christmas Eve bombing of Hanoi brought international condemnation. Soon virtually no college or university in the United States was without an organized student movement, often led by the left-wing Students for a Democratic Society (SDS) or allied groups.

During the 1960s, the University of Wisconsin–Madison gained a reputation as one of the nation's most radical campuses. Students and professors began to organize teach-ins on the war in 1965. The teach-ins were large forums for discussion between students and faculty about the war. Students marched to protest the Vietnam War, burned draft cards, and confronted army recruiters. In October 1967 University of Wisconsin students protested against the Dow Chemical Company, makers of the weapon napalm, who were recruiting at the Madison campus. The resulting police action and violent confrontation helped to radicalize many formerly apolitical students. The October riot was part of an anti-Dow protest that had begun months before the company's representatives arrived on campus and would have long-lasting effects.

THE STERLING HALL BOMBING

Another, more disturbing event took place on campus on August 24, 1970. Early that morning, four young men drove to campus in a stolen Ford Econoline van filled with close to two thousand pounds of ammonium nitrate topped with fuel oil. They parked the van next to Sterling Hall. At 3:42 a.m., shortly after they lit the fuse, the bomb exploded, destroying a large portion of Sterling Hall. The bomb injured four men inside the building and killed Robert Fassnacht, a promising young physicist.

The bombers, Karl Armstrong, Dwight Armstrong, David Fine, and Leo Burt, were members of the New Year's Gang, an antiwar group that demonstrated its opposition through property damage.

WHi Image ID 33884

Sterling Hall in the aftermath of the bombing

They had targeted Sterling Hall because it housed the Army Mathematics Research Center, an Army-funded facility that many protesters believed contributed to the death and destruction in Vietnam. The four had not intended to injure, much less kill, anyone; they planted the bomb on a Monday morning when school was not in session and notified the police in advance. Unfortunately, things did not go as planned. While many feared that the bombing would escalate tensions and encourage more violent protest, Sterling Hall and the sobering impact of Fassnacht's death brought a sudden halt to the violence. A calmer mood spread, one that deterred extreme violence in the name of peace, and until the Oklahoma City bombing of 1995, Sterling Hall remained the largest act of domestic sabotage.

Ultimately, the United States failed to achieve its goal of propping up the government of South Vietnam. Instead, the North Vietnamese and Vietcong forces managed to occupy more and more territory in the South. The opponents' successes, combined with growing voter disenchantment with the war in the United States, prompted the government to start peace negotiations, which were signed in January of 1973; U.S. troops were withdrawn two months later. The end of hostilities finally came in April of 1975, when Saigon (now called Ho Chi Minh City) fell to Communist forces. Vietnam reunified under Communist control as the Socialist Republic of Vietnam.

19

GREENING WISCONSIN

"THAT THE GREAT FOREST, and the Forest Trees of our country, are worthy of much more attention, not only from the cultivator, but also from the artisan, and even the statesman, is evident to every one who bestows upon them a thought . . . Few persons can realize its extent, or the amount we owe to the native forests of our country for the capital and wealth our people are now enjoying." So wrote Increase Lapham in 1858, long before anyone else had given much thought to the value of the natural world.

THE EARLY ENVIRONMENTAL MOVEMENT

Concern for the environment emerged as a complex and broadly popular political and cultural movement in the United States in the late nineteenth century, waxing and waning through the succeeding decades before coming to a fever pitch in the 1970s that continues to increase to this day. Newly urbanized Americans were becoming increasingly aware of the importance of nature as an economic, aesthetic, and spiritual resource, especially as they became convinced that nature's resources were imperiled by industrialization. This movement led to unprecedented public and private initiatives to ensure the conservation of natural resources and the preservation of wildlife and land. By the turn of the twentieth century, Wisconsin had become a center of conservation thinking and activity in the United States.

Increase Lapham (the same person who also first systematically investigated Indian mounds) is generally considered the founder of the Wisconsin conservation movement. Arriving in Milwaukee three days before Wisconsin became a territory in 1836, Lapham kept careful records on the environment that served as models for those who followed him. In the 1850s, when Henry David Thoreau and George Perkins Marsh were advocating similar concepts in New England, Lapham began to argue for an ecological point of view toward the Wisconsin frontier. In 1855 he urged the state legislature to authorize a natural history survey before any more of Wisconsin's native species became extinct under the brunt of white settlement and industrialization. He also warned about the devastation of state forests, fifty years before it became an issue of national importance. Lapham's 1867 book *Report on the Disastrous Effects of the Destruction of Forest Trees, Now Going on So Rapidly in the State of Wisconsin* was one of the first to stress the importance of natural resources. He wrote other books about the state's native grasses and Indian effigy mounds.

Increase Lapham, Wisconsin's first conservationist and the nineteenth century's foremost scientist, examines a fragment of a 33-pound meteorite found in Trenton, Wisconsin, in 1871.

WHi Image ID 1944

Also in the 1850s, the man who would become the best-known environmental thinker of Wisconsin and the nation was immersed in farm chores near Portage. Though he would achieve his greatest fame for his years in California, John Muir spent his formative years in Wisconsin. In 1849 the Muir family immigrated to the United States from Scotland. Until he entered the University of Wisconsin in 1861, Muir worked from dawn to dusk on his family farm, roaming the fields and woods whenever he was allowed a short period away from the plow. Muir was also an inventor, creating a desk that rotated his schoolbooks after a preset time studying as well as an alarm clock that would tip up his bed and dump him on the floor at the appointed time; he showed this "early-rising machine" at the 1860 Wisconsin State Fair. Muir later wrote that his strenuous years in Wisconsin's outdoors prepared him for his later wilderness ramblings.

CONSERVATION EFFORTS

In the second half of the nineteenth century, as lumberjacks swept across the central and northern portions of our state, saving some of Wisconsin's forests from the lumber industry was one motivation for the creation of the first state parks. In 1878 the legislature approved The State Park, a 760-square mile state area in northern Wisconsin. The proposal was ill-fated from the start: the state owned just 10 percent of the total land within the area's boundaries and the population was too small to support the project. Lumber barons who opposed the park's provisions were the primary power brokers in the region, and the state eventually sold two-thirds of its land to private interests in 1897.

At the turn of the twentieth century, Robert M. La Follette's Progressive politics influenced the rise of conservation concerns on the state level. Rebelling against the political influence of the lumber barons, La Follette led the fight to protect Wisconsin's natural resources from complete economic exploitation. He also worked closely with professors at the University of Wisconsin, including geologist and university president (1903–18) Charles Van Hise. Van Hise chaired the State Conservation Commission, provided conservation advice to Teddy Roosevelt, and wrote the first textbook on conservation in 1910.

In these early years of land conservation, the creation of each new state park required separate legislative action. The first State Park Board was appointed in 1907. John Nolen, a noted landscape architect, was hired to draft a feasibility plan for a state park system. Nolen's report, published by the State Park Board, provided guidelines for a park system and recommended the creation of four state parks: Devil's Lake, the Dells of the Wisconsin River, Fish Creek in Door County, and at the confluence of the Mississippi and Wisconsin Rivers. All but the Dells of the Wisconsin River became state parks soon after. In 1915 the State Park Board merged with the State Board of Forestry, the Fisheries Commission, and the State Game Warden Department to form the State Conservation Commission.

Forest conservation was also essential to Wisconsin's Indian populations. For centuries the Menominee had practiced extensive forest management, even as logging became a major industry and source of income for the tribe in the nineteenth century. Unlike many other areas of the state, the forests on the Menominee reservation were not clear-cut and burned. Today the Menominee are known worldwide for their sustainable forestry practices, maintaining forestland on 220,000 of their 235,000 acres.

NEW ENVIRONMENTAL GOALS

These early conservation efforts inspired a later generation of Wisconsin environmentalists, who would breathe new life into the movement and introduce new goals for protecting the state's and the world's resources in the twentieth century. While the conservation movement had stressed natural resources as commodities to produce material goods and thus called for more efficient management of both renewable and nonrenewable resources, the environmental movement grew out of interest in outdoor recreation and focused on resources—air, water, and land—to enhance the quality of life. Rather than focusing on the efficient development of exploitable resources, the environmental movement prized these same resources for aesthetic, moral, or spiritual reasons.

One of the most notable figures of the modern environmental movement was Aldo Leopold, who inspired many environmentalists to appreciate wildlife and to use the land sensibly and sensitively. Born in Iowa in 1887, Leopold developed many of his insights while spending time at his family cabin, known as the "shack," near Baraboo. He carefully observed and recorded every detail of the plants and animals around him, recognizing how everything in nature was connected. Serving on the Wisconsin Conservation Commission in the 1940s, Leopold helped to formulate policies that emphasized the management of land not just for commercial uses but also for the benefit of humans, animals, and plants. Leopold's most famous book, *A Sand County Almanac* (1949), was published a year after his death and contains short essays describing a year spent in his Wisconsin River shack. Leopold's work helped give rise to a new attitude toward wildlife—as an object of observation rather than of sport hunting.

Leopold's ideas characterized the shift toward preservation, appreciation, and protection of nature that dominated the emerging environmental movement in the 1940s and 1950s. This new perspective on animals and natural resources ultimately led to the federal Endangered Species Act, state-sponsored wildlife programs, a heightened interest in habitats for plants and animals, and a focus on biological diversity. The environmental movement's emphasis on the preservation of specific resources in a more natural environment led to the creation of the National Wilderness Preservation System in 1964 and the National Trails System in 1968 as well as to a public purchase program in the Land and Water Conservation Act of 1964.

In the 1960s Governor Gaylord Nelson established a national reputation as a leader in environmental protection with his advocacy of Wisconsin's pioneering Outdoor Recreation Act (1961). The act pledged $50 million over the next decade toward environmental planning, land acquisition, and easements along state highways to ensure scenic values. Elected to the U.S. Senate in 1962, Nelson proposed a constitutional amendment that stated, "Every person has the inalienable right to a decent environment." In a 1969 speech in Seattle, Nelson borrowed a tactic of the anti-Vietnam war protests—the

WHi Image ID 56854

Gaylord Nelson canoes at the Apostle Islands, which he authored legislation to protect.

teach-in; he suggested a full day of teaching and learning about the environment. Nelson believed that if people knew more about the environment, they would take better care of it and demand better protection. His efforts led to the first Earth Day on April 22, 1970.

In response to Nelson's efforts, Congress created the Environmental Protection Agency (EPA) to repair existing environmental damage and to establish policies to keep the environment safe and clean. It also passed the Water Quality Improvement Act and the Air Quality Control Act.

HISTORIC PRESERVATION

At the same time that conservation of natural resources rose to the national agenda, a parallel movement, one concerned with the preservation of cultural resources and historic landscapes, was also growing. In 1966 Congress passed the National Historic Preservation Act, which gave the federal government a leadership role in the preservation of archaeological sites and historic buildings, structures, and objects. Among its many provisions, the act established the National Register of Historic Places, encouraged the creation of State Historic Preservation Offices, and defined the provision that federal preservation programs would rely on the voluntary cooperation of property owners and would not interfere with ownership rights. The act marked the climax of a series of efforts around the nation to protect historic sites and landscapes that began in the nineteenth century with the preservation of Philadelphia's Independence Hall and George Washington's Mount Vernon. The moving of a pioneer cabin in Antigo in 1914 marked one of the first conscious efforts to save a historic building in Wisconsin.

Archaeologist and historian Charles E. Brown was a leader and innovator in historic preservation before it even existed as a discipline. Alarmed at the destruction of Indian mounds occurring throughout the state in the early 1900s, Brown urged the Wisconsin Archaeological Society, which he had founded and where he served as editor and secretary, to make the preservation of the mounds a top priority. The plan he helped them develop became Wisconsin's first historic preservation movement, involving surveys, protective legislation, public acquisition and stewardship, partnerships, fundraising, creation of landmarks, and relentless promotion and education. Working with the Landmarks Committee of the Federated Women's Clubs of Wisconsin, the Daughters of the American Revolution, local historical societies, and other public-service organizations, the Wisconsin Archaeological Society placed historic markers on mound groups across the state to call public attention to these important ancient structures. In 1911 Brown spearheaded the effort that led to the passage of a state law to protect antiquities on public lands—Wisconsin's first historic preservation law.

As the twentieth century progressed, archaeologists and historic preservationists became strong supporters of efforts to protect the environment through public and private land acquisition, recognizing that the creation of "natural areas" and conservation parks also offered protection to the archaeological and cultural sites contained within these landscapes.

As governor, Gaylord Nelson also made it explicitly clear that concern for the environment included the built environment as well. Rundown neighborhoods and decayed buildings became "blighted environments" that could be cleaned up, recycled, and reused, creating historic neighborhoods out of existing infrastructure and revitalizing communities, particularly in rural areas. To encourage the reuse of older buildings, the federal government introduced a tax credit program for the rehabilitation of historic structures in 1976 that has returned more than $1 billion to Wisconsin home and business owners since its inception.

Wisconsin waterways have been the focus of many more recent environmental projects and debates. Dams built by lumber companies to store logs in the late nineteenth and early twentieth centuries have been removed from many rivers, restoring natural wildlife and plants as well as aiding the economic revitalization of waterfront communities. The removal of polychlorinated biphenyls, or PCBs, from the Fox River, however, has proved more contentious. The federal government banned the manufacture of PCBs in 1977, but the toxic chemicals remained in the soil long after their release by seven paper companies. Despite the known health risks associated with PCBs, differing cleanup efforts and goals have divided the EPA, the Department of Natural Resources, and environmental organizations.

Wisconsin has long placed a priority on environmental health and safety. The voluntary Green Tier Law, for example, rewards environmental performance that goes beyond the minimum standards required by law for air, water, land, and natural resources. Green Tier allows the state to distinguish between good environmental performers and those performing at or near the regulatory minimums and provides incentives for businesses to improve their existing environmental programs. In 2007 Wisconsin launched the statewide initiative Travel Green Wisconsin, the first ecotourism certification program in the nation, which recognizes travel-related businesses that have taken specific actions toward environmental, social, and economic sustainability. Other programs, like the Wisconsin Environmental Education Board, provide Wisconsin citizens with additional ways to maintain the state's long history of citizen involvement in environmental education, leadership, and reform, all of which Increase Lapham had first advocated in the state's infancy.

20

THE CHANGING FACE
OF IMMIGRATION

WISCONSIN'S STATE DANCE arrived ringing in the heads of the Europeans who came in the second great wave of immigration during the late nineteenth and early twentieth centuries. The polka had originated as a Czech peasant dance and swept the dance halls of Europe in the 1840s. Polish American immigrants then adopted the polka, and as their numbers increased in Wisconsin, the state could scarcely resist being overtaken by the sounds of stomping feet and a rollicking accordion melody.

From the late nineteenth century through the end of World War II, immigration policy in the United States underwent dramatic changes that helped to alter both the pace and the face of immigration. High rates of immigration in the nineteenth century sparked nativist sentiment and encouraged the introduction of restrictive legislation, particularly toward immigrants from Asia. Two world wars and the Great Depression only intensified nativist and anti-immigration forces as numerous bills in Congress advocated the suspension of immigration and even the deportation of non-Americans. Deportation became a particularly common theme after the Russian Revolution of 1917, when fears of Communism caused some to advocate for the removal of people with what many considered subversive political beliefs, primarily socialism.

EUROPEAN IMMIGRANTS

At the beginning of the twentieth century, a rapidly industrializing economy ushered in a new wave of immigrants to the United States. This fresh group of European immigrants arrived from the east and the south. Whereas the mid- to late nineteenth century had brought Irish, Norwegians, and Germans, now Poles, Russians, and Italians began coming in increasing numbers to Wisconsin.

Czechs were some of the earliest eastern Europeans to come to Wisconsin, settling along Lake Michigan and in the north, where they often worked in the lumber industry or established small farms in the cutover. Russians and Slovaks arrived later, settling primarily in the more urban locales of Milwaukee, Kenosha, and Racine, where they worked as industrial laborers. While many Russians arrived in the 1890s, a large number also immigrated in the 1940s, along with a number of Holocaust survivors seeking political asylum. The fall of Communism in the Soviet Union in 1989 allowed thousands of eastern Europeans, particularly Russian Jews, to leave their homelands for the first time in over sixty years.

After Germans, Poles are now the largest ethnic group in Wisconsin. They did not begin immigrating in large numbers until the twentieth century, however, pushed by political oppression and poverty at home. The first major Polish settlement in Wisconsin (and one of the earliest in the United States) was established around 1862, a few miles from Stevens Point in central Wisconsin. Named Polonia, the settlement attracted a largely farming population of Poles, most of whom had worked as farmers and laborers in Poland. Many men also worked in Wisconsin's lumber camps in the winter, leaving their wives and children to clear the land while they were away.

In the 1850s Poles began settling in Milwaukee, where they worked as unskilled laborers. Polish men established the Milwaukee Society to promote American citizenship among Poles and to preserve Polish cultural traditions. Polish women could belong to the Ladies Auxiliary. The Society began publishing a newsletter in 1932 to inform members of community activities and to attract new members.

Prior to 1900 few Italians and Greeks lived in the state, but economic hardships in the early decades of the century in Europe led many to seek a better life in Wisconsin. Settling primarily in the industrial southeast, many Greek and Italian immigrants intended to stay only long enough to earn money to purchase land back home. In the end, however, most remained, establishing distinct ethnic neighborhoods in cities throughout southern Wisconsin, such as the Greenbush neighborhood in Madison.

HISPANIC IMMIGRANTS

Hispanic Americans have been in Wisconsin since before statehood, but they did not become a sizable population until the 1950s. Prior to that, most Hispanics in Wisconsin were Mexicans working as migrant laborers recruited by manufacturers and agricultural contractors to fill labor shortages caused by labor strikes and immigration laws restricting the number of European immigrants. Most were not in Wisconsin by choice but were displaced by the economic aftereffects of the 1910 Mexican Revolution. By 1925 around nine thousand Mexican Americans lived in Milwaukee, but most lost their jobs during the Depression and moved back home. The Hispanic immigrants who stayed struggled under restrictive government programs and inadequate community services.

During World War II, labor shortfalls led the United States to create the Emergency Farm Labor Program. Agricultural employers brought in male workers from Jamaica, the Bahamas, British Honduras, and Mexico. The labor shortage also inspired desperate measures. In 1944 the United States started sending German prisoners of war to America to work. More than thirteen thousand German prisoners worked in the fields of Wisconsin's thirty-eight POW camps.

After the war, Mexican farm laborers continued to come north under the federal "Bracero" program, an agreement between the

United States and Mexico for the temporary migration of Mexican workers that lasted from 1942 to 1964. Braceros were mostly single, male, experienced farm workers who hailed from regions such as Coahuila and other crucial agricultural regions in Mexico. More than four million Mexicans left their own lands and families, chasing the rumor of economic boom in the United States. It was by the work of their hands that the United States became a global agricultural center.

Industrial jobs in Milwaukee, Kenosha, and Racine counties brought more Mexicans to Wisconsin in the 1950s, where they found both an established Mexican community and work that was relatively safe. But in rural Wisconsin, thousands of agricultural workers lacked the basic protections gained by factory workers in the Progressive era. Wages, child labor, length of workdays, and other basic concerns

WHi Image ID 22900

A Mexican woman and her six children on the porch of the multi-family housing provided by the pea cannery where her husband and father work in Plymouth

went unregulated in the fields, and standards of living fell far below the state average. In 1950 the Governor's Commission on Human Rights issued a report on the living and working conditions of migratory laborers in Wisconsin. They found that because of their transitory life, migrant workers often went unnoticed by public officials and, in addition to other forms of discrimination, suffered from sickness, poor sanitation, inadequate housing, and low wages. Conditions weren't much better in the cities. A 1971 investigation of urban Hispanic communities found them to be among the state's poorest, with the least access to quality housing, education, or health care. Racial discrimination and language barriers were not the only reasons for this situation, however, as investigators concluded that state and local agencies charged with advocating for Hispanic citizens had mostly failed. In the early 1970s mechanical harvesting and processing equipment reduced the need for migrant labor; from a high of about 15,000 in 1955, their numbers dropped to 6,000 in 1970. Mexicans, either straight from Mexico or from the Rio Grande Valley in south Texas, still constitute the largest group of migratory workers in Wisconsin.

Today, Hispanics are the fastest growing ethnic group in Wisconsin, more than doubling in size from 1990 to 2000. Attracted by jobs or perhaps deciding to remain permanently after long periods of seasonal labor, people of Hispanic origin are settling in Wisconsin communities large and small, bringing—often abruptly in smaller towns—new racial and ethnic diversification. Mexicans comprise nearly 72 percent of the total Hispanic population, though Puerto Ricans are another fast-growing group. Wisconsin has also become home to political refugees and a scattering of other immigrants from Cuba, El Salvador, Colombia, and Nicaragua.

ASIAN IMMIGRANTS

Along with Hispanics, Asians are another relatively "recent" immigrant group. Wisconsin received little Asian immigration in the nineteenth century, particularly after the United States eliminated direct immigration from China (in 1882), India (in 1917), Japan (in 1924), and the Philippines (in 1934). (During World War II, some Japanese, many of whom were American citizens, were interned at Camp McCoy, today's Fort McCoy, near Sparta in Monroe County.) The 1965 Immigration and Nationality Act removed immigration restrictions based on national origins in favor of a preference system that gave priority to family reunification and political refugees. Most Asian immigration to Wisconsin has occurred in recent decades, particularly among Hmong refugees from Laos.

Recruited during the Vietnam War as guerrilla soldiers to fight the North Vietnamese, Hmong peoples literally lived in the crossfire during the conflict. When the United States withdrew from Vietnam in 1975, the Hmong who had aided the United States were left in the hands of the Communists they had fought. Thousands fled to refugee camps in Thailand, where resettlement organizations, such as the U.S. Catholic Conference and Lutheran Immigration and Refugee Services, helped to sponsor Hmong immigration to the United States beginning in 1975. After Minnesota and California, Wisconsin has the third largest Hmong population in the country. The largest communities in Wisconsin are in La Crosse, Sheboygan, Green Bay, Wausau, and Milwaukee.

Like other immigrants, Hmong refugees faced many challenges adjusting to American culture, particularly racist and prejudicial attitudes. Numerous state and community organizations attempted to educate Wisconsinites on Hmong culture and the Hmong on American culture. At a meeting held by La Crosse assemblyman John Medinger in July 1991, nineteen Hmong women shared stories about their racial interactions in the community. They reported being repeatedly sworn at, threatened, and labeled with racial epithets.

Some Wisconsinites, like many white Americans, are troubled by these new groups, even if those who are fearful are not themselves under any particular threat. Mexican Wisconsinites who have lived in the state for generations are sometimes presumed to be illegal immigrants, while other immigrants are presumed to be living off the

WHi Image ID 7196

Children from a variety of backgrounds celebrate Ethnic Pride Day at a church in Milwaukee.

state's generosity. In letters to the editors in newspapers around the state, many whites express fear for the future of the state and the country, perhaps forgetting that their own European ancestors may also have appeared unwilling to assimilate or resisted learning English more than a century ago. Wisconsin's future will be determined by what the state's Germans, Norwegians, Poles, Irish, African Americans, Mexicans, Hmong, Indians, and others create together.

21

INDIAN
TREATY RIGHTS

ALTHOUGH WISCONSIN'S STATE FISH is the much-desired mus-
kellunge, it was the walleye that came to symbolize the fight over
the right to fish in the late twentieth century. The issue of treaty
rights exploded in northern Wisconsin in the late 1980s, as more and
more members of Ojibwe tribes began to test the meaning of hunting and fishing rights granted to them by the U.S. government in
treaties made in the nineteenth century.

SOVEREIGNTY

By the mid-twentieth century, Wisconsin's Indian communities had
experienced nearly one hundred years of post-treaty life, much of
it spent in dispute with the federal and state governments. The U.S.
Constitution guaranteed the tribes' sovereignty (the right to be self-
governing), but throughout history the actual status of Indian tribes
had been contested. Federal officials had confined Indians to reservations, tried to assimilate them into mainstream society through
schools and land allotments, and encouraged tribes to form tribal
governments to conduct their own internal affairs.

As members of sovereign nations, Indians are both United States
citizens and citizens of their tribes. Like other Americans, Indians
are subject to federal laws. They are not always subject to state laws,
however, because Indian reservations are held in trust by the federal

government. A government-to-government relationship exists between the U.S. government and each sovereign tribe that is certified as a federally recognized tribal government.

Today, eleven federally recognized Indian tribes call Wisconsin home: the Bad River Band of the Lake Superior Chippewa, Forest County Potawatomi, Lac Courte Oreilles Band of Lake Superior Chippewa, Lac du Flambeau Band of Lake Superior Chippewa, Menominee, Oneida, Red Cliff Band of Lake Superior Chippewa, St. Croix Chippewa, Sokaogon Chippewa, Stockbridge Munsee, and the Ho-Chunk. (The Brothertown tribe filed a petition for recognition in 1996 but has yet to receive federal recognition of its tribal rights and sovereignty.)

As waves of white settlers moved west in the early nineteenth century, many Indians had found it increasingly difficult to maintain their status as independent nations because the United States did little to protect their rights. In 1832 Chief Justice John Marshall defined the limits of Indian sovereignty in the case of *Worcester v. Georgia*. Marshall maintained that Indian tribes had been treated as independent and sovereign nations since the arrival of Europeans but that the various treaties that put tribes under the protection of the United States had terminated their status as independent nations. Marshall called them instead "domestic dependent nations," a term that signified the tribes' right to regulate internal tribal affairs while precluding their making agreements with any nation other than the United States. The United States continued to make treaties with Indian tribes until 1871, when the federal government began negotiating formal agreements that required congressional approval. Additionally, treaties only required Senate approval, and the House of Representatives wanted some say in the process.

ASSIMILATION EFFORTS

One of the reasons for discontinuing the use of treaties was that they were seen as impediments to the assimilation of Indians into white society. To encourage assimilation, Congress passed the General Allotment Act of 1887 (also known as the Dawes Act), which transferred the communal ownership of tribal lands to individual ownership of eighty-acre parcels. Instead of land belonging to the tribe as a whole, tribal land was broken up and given to individuals—the white model of land ownership. After the allotment process was completed, the federal government sold the "excess" land to whites, with the intention of exposing Indians to the "civilizing" effects of mainstream American society. Allotment proved a dismal failure, depriving formerly nomadic Indians of hunting lands, weakening the social structure of many tribes, and confining Indians to reservations that came to be characterized by poverty and disease. By the time it ended in 1934, tribes like the Ojibwe had lost more than 40 percent of their homelands.

Federal courts did not always agree with John Marshall's delineation of Indian sovereignty, and by the twentieth century the legal status of Indians was in a state of disarray. All Indians were given U.S. citizenship in 1924, when they received a form of dual citizenship with their tribal citizenship. Previously, only Indians who had met certain guidelines could become citizens. In 1934 Congress passed the Indian Reorganization Act (IRA). This reversed the federal government's fifty-year-old policy of Indian assimilation, which had tried to force Indians to give up their languages, cultures, and identity in favor of white culture. The IRA encouraged tribes to form their own governments and to conduct their own internal affairs. These new tribal governments drafted constitutions and provided tribes with political bodies that could assert their sovereign rights.

TERMINATION

In the 1950s critics of Indian self-determination instigated an ill-conceived federal effort to dismantle the reservation system and free the U.S. government from the costs of protecting Indians and their property. Passed in 1953, House Concurrent Resolution 108 laid out the goals of "termination and relocation," a policy intended to encourage the movement of Indians from rural reservations to urban areas through job training programs and housing assistance. Unfortunately, most Wisconsin Indians who opted for relocation received nothing more than a one-way bus ticket to Chicago, Milwaukee, or St. Paul.

Termination policy ended federal recognition of more than fifty tribal governments. The Menominee were one of the first tribes to undergo termination, singled out because the federal government felt that they possessed the economic resources to succeed without government support and supervision. On April 30, 1961, the reservation ceased to exist, becoming instead Menominee County. A new corporate body, Menominee Enterprises Inc., began to oversee the tribe's financial assets and property. Termination brought tremendous social costs to the tribe, which, without federal funds, was forced to close its hospital and lay off mill workers to increase profits. In 1970 a grassroots activist group formed to try to end termination and restore Menominee status as a federally recognized tribe—Determination of Rights and Unity for Menominee Shareholders (DRUMS). The group succeeded. In April of 1975 the county reverted back to reservation status, and the Menominee were again eligible to receive the services and support of the U.S. Department of Interior Indian Affairs.

TREATY RIGHTS AND SPEARFISHING

In the 1970s off-reservation treaty rights became a particularly controversial issue when two brothers from the Lac Courte Oreilles band of Ojibwe were arrested for off-reservation spearfishing. While many courts had addressed unregulated hunting and fishing over the years, it was not until 1983 that the United States Supreme Court upheld a lower court ruling that favored the Ojibwe. Known as the Voigt Decision, the ruling confirmed that the 1837 and 1842

A cartoon depicting the conflict over treaty rights

treaties between the United States and the Ojibwe had guaranteed Ojibwe rights to hunt and fish off-reservation without regulation by the State of Wisconsin. In 1984 the Great Lakes Indian Fish and Wildlife Commission was formed to educate the public and to assist tribes in implementing and protecting these treaty rights.

Many non-Indians in northern Wisconsin rejected the Voigt Decision, however, believing that it permitted the Ojibwe to take most, if not all, of the state's mandated "safe harvest" allotment of walleye from several lakes. Some feared that spearfishing would effectively close those bodies of water for sport fishing and result in severe damage to the tourism industry. Others objected to the Ojibwe tradition of spear-fishing during the walleye spawning season, claiming that the practice would reduce the number of walleye for sport fishing in northern lakes. Organizations like Stop Treaty Abuse Wisconsin (STA-W) and Protect Americans' Rights and Resources

(PARR) mobilized their members to protest off-reservation hunting and spearfishing.

The Ojibwe traditionally spearfished at night, using torches to attract fish to their canoes, where the fishermen could spear them. Modern Ojibwe employed the same basic technique, but added equipment like electric headlamps, metal spearheads, and motorized aluminum boats.

Confrontations between Indians and non-Indians became increasingly violent, aggressive, and sometimes outright racist as the Ojibwe won additional legal support for their spearfishing rights

WHi Image ID 35211

Indian children at a Lac Courte Oreilles Band of Lake Superior Chippewa demonstration against a proposed dam on the Chippewa Flowage in Chippewa Falls in 1971

during the 1980s. Because spearfishers had to launch their motor-boats from lake landings, these spots became a prime target for the anti-spearfishing protestors. Protestors also used larger motorboats to disrupt Ojibwe fishing on the water itself, leading to many dangerous encounters.

Tensions peaked in 1989. Earlier that year, STA-W had urged its constituency "to use every available means to minimize the slaughter of spawning Wisconsin sport fish" by Ojibwe spearfish-ers. As part of this effort, STA-W sponsored a contest to find the best concrete walleye decoys, which they intended to mass produce to foil spear-fishers. Among the requirements were that decoys had to "have flat bottoms," "reflective eyes," and "be made of concrete at least 2 inches thick." In response, some Ojibwe announced a contest of their own, offering a $100 reward to the first Indian to retrieve a concrete walleye from a lake. Rumors also circulated among the Ojibwe that PARR members had placed explosives inside some of the concrete walleyes. Although no evidence of booby-trapped decoys was uncovered, the rumor exemplified the level of harassment, intimidation, and violence that the protests unleashed.

Under Governor Tommy Thompson, the State of Wisconsin re-quested an injunction to prohibit Ojibwe spearfishing in order to prevent further violence. On May 5, 1989, federal Judge Barbara Crabb refused the request and chastised the state for attempting to avoid violence by punishing the Ojibwe, who had broken no laws. Over the next couple years, however, Crabb did rule several times to restrict Ojibwe off-reservation rights, including their right to har-vest timber for commercial purposes from public lands.

On May 20, 1991, the State of Wisconsin declared that it would no longer attempt to appeal the 1983 Voigt Decision. The cessation of legal challenges, coupled with injunctions against some of the more militant anti-spearfishing protestors, helped dampen protests. The Ojibwe agreed to limits on spearfishing harvests and increased tribal efforts to stock and preserve fish and game populations. By the mid-1990s, relative peace had returned to northern Wisconsin.

GAMING

Apart from treaty rights, the most significant modern issue related to tribal sovereignty came with the expansion of gambling in 1987. Gambling had been prohibited before Wisconsin even became a state, and the state constitution expressly forbade the legislature from authorizing any lottery, which courts had interpreted broadly to mean any type of gambling. Local governments were often unwilling to enforce the law, however, and until 1945, when strict anti-gambling laws were passed, slot machines, punchboards, numbers jars, and other gambling devices were popular in taverns, private clubs, and resorts. Even after stricter laws were enacted, gambling remained a controversial political issue, and in 1965, 1973, and 1977 Wisconsin voters overwhelmingly approved constitutional amendments that allowed residents to participate in certain types of promotional contests, charitable bingo, and charitable raffles. Ten years later, in 1987, a statewide referendum approved the creation of a state lottery. By not expressly prohibiting other forms of gambling, it also inadvertently gave Wisconsin tribes the right to establish casino-type gambling, including blackjack, roulette, and slot machines. Many tribes, including the Ho-Chunk, Ojibwe, Mohican, and Potawatomi, have opened casinos that provide substantial economic benefits to reservation communities.

POSTWAR POLITICS
AND THE
CONSERVATIVE
REVOLUTION

As Wisconsin's economy expanded in the 1950s and 1960s, the state's industries diversified, cities flourished, suburbs sprouted on land that had once grown corn and raised cattle, and the state's political landscape shifted. With the demise of the Progressive Party in 1946, the Democratic Party received an infusion of progressivism, which became the base on which the Democrats built their party and power in the postwar era. Former Progressive leaders and New Deal Democrats engineered victories in local elections throughout the 1950s, challenging Wisconsin's long-standing Republican majority and seriously contending for power for the first time since the nineteenth century. When Democrat William Proxmire won a special 1957 election to fill the seat of Senator Joseph McCarthy, it signaled a change in Wisconsin politics that reflected the increasing political power of the state's urban populations. The election of Democrat Gaylord Nelson as governor in 1958 and then senator in 1962 confirmed that—buoyed by organized labor and dissatisfaction with Republican farm policies—the party had achieved statewide support. In 1965 Democrats gained a majority in the state assembly for only the second time since the 1930s.

Such a political transformation did not happen frequently. A century earlier, in the 1850s, the Republican Party had emerged from the chaotic and divisive politics of the antebellum era and risen to dominance. Wisconsin's Progressives broke with the Republicans to establish their own independent party between 1934 and 1946. But in the years following World War II, Wisconsin abandoned its longtime penchant for one-party and three-party politics to the join the American two-party mainstream.

As Wisconsin Democrats reached their electoral peak in the 1970s, another political shift began to take shape in response to a changing world. Postwar economic prosperity gave way to sluggish economic growth and inflation, and a new generation of conservative leaders with different ideas about the role and place of government in daily life rose to power.

THE CALL FOR SMALLER GOVERNMENT

The 1970s inflicted several blows to American confidence. The Watergate crisis, coupled with the divisiveness that led to the withdrawal from Vietnam in 1975, shattered people's trust in the presidency. The national rise of the service sector at the expense of industry and manufacturing contributed to rising unemployment and economic recession throughout the Northeast and Midwest—traditional strongholds of industry and manufacturing. To make matters worse, the Organization of Petroleum Exporting Countries (OPEC) began showing its strength by banding together to limit oil sales to the United States and Europe, driving up the cost of oil and sending the U.S. economy into a tailspin.

As prices and wages rose, taxpayers who had funded two decades of liberal government programs began to revolt. President John F. Kennedy's New Frontier—a program intended to boost the economy, provide social welfare, and set cold war policies—and Lyndon Johnson's Great Society—a program aimed at eliminating poverty and racial injustice—had created costly bureaucracies that seemed to have produced more red tape than solutions. Against this backdrop of perceived American decline and rising prices, conservative politicians began dismantling expensive federal programs and removing government regulations on business, ending half a century of liberal assumptions about the proper role of government in American life. By 1980 taxpayers, alarmed at rising prices and frustrated by red tape, agreed with Ronald Reagan when he said, "Government is not a solution to our problem; government is the problem," and elected Reagan to decrease the size of the government and increase accountability.

Former Wisconsin governor Tommy Thompson

WHi Image ID 70982

In Wisconsin, Tommy Thompson carried the banner of conservative revolt by focusing on revitalizing the state's economy and reforming welfare. Elected to his first term as governor in 1986, Thompson went on to dominate state politics for fourteen years, becoming Wisconsin's longest-serving governor. He championed—even led the way on—many Reagan and George H. W. Bush administration priorities.

WELFARE REFORM

Echoing Reagan's criticisms of the nation's welfare program, in 1987 Thompson sponsored changes to the state program that increased the responsibilities of welfare recipients. The state's Learnfare program, for example, required welfare recipients to send their children to school. In 1995 the "Work Not Welfare" program required welfare recipients to work and placed time limits on their benefits.

In 1997 Wisconsin replaced its Aid to Families with Dependent Children program with Wisconsin Works, or W-2, which became a national model for welfare reform. Characterizing the program as "employment rather than welfare," Thompson's program encouraged people to break their welfare dependency by providing opportunities for individuals to find gainful employment through further education. W-2 provided families with money for both schooling and childcare on the condition that recipients find work within five years. Under W-2, Wisconsin reduced its welfare caseload by 93 percent. Although W-2 succeeded in doing exactly what it intended, critics contended that recipients often ended up in service-sector jobs that did not pay enough to support a family.

In addition to welfare reform, in 1990 Thompson created the nation's first school choice program. School choice allowed low-income Milwaukee families to send their children to the public or private school of their choice. Thompson also introduced Wisconsin's Council on Model Academic Standards, a forerunner to the national No Child Left Behind Act, which imposed high academic standards in language arts, math, science, and social studies on all students.

Thompson also worked to remedy one of the weaknesses of W-2 by extending healthcare benefits to low-income and disabled people. His BadgerCare program, formally launched in 1999, provided health insurance to uninsured families, and had enrolled more than 77,000 people by 2000. Wisconsin's Pathways to Independence was the nation's first program to ensure the continuance of health benefits for disabled individuals who entered the workforce, providing easy access to a system of service and benefits counseling. Another health program, FamilyCare, allowed elderly and disabled citizens to receive care in their homes as long as needed.

Wisconsin's experiment in offering public insurance coverage to low-income, uninsured individuals and families drew the interest of both state and federal policymakers. The President's Council of Economic Advisors noted in 2000 that "direct provision of health insurance through public programs is the most efficient way of targeting low-income families." Policymakers have also been impressed with the comprehensive benefit package offered to its enrollees.

Unlike other legislative initiatives, BadgerCare and its associated programs represented truly collaborative efforts between Republicans and Democrats. While they may have differed on the structure, all agreed on the programs' importance.

Early in 2001, Thompson resigned the governorship to become Secretary of Health and Human Services for the Bush administration and was succeeded by his Lieutenant Governor Scott McCallum. Although McCallum lost his campaign to Democrat James Doyle in 2002, Republicans remained in control of both houses of the state legislature and continued to exert a powerful hold on the state's politics into the twenty-first century.

At the time of this writing, Wisconsin's—and the country's—political climate seems once more torn between Republicans and Democrats, much as it was after World War II. Disagreement continues between parties and citizens over how to address issues such as economic upheaval, climate change, and the ongoing U.S. wars in Afghanistan and Iraq. No one party dominates the state, as Wisconsin, and the nation, works to find its place and direction in a new century.

CONCLUSION

Creating Wisconsin

I had never been to Wisconsin, but all my life I had heard about it, had eaten its cheeses, some of them as good as any in the world. And I must have seen pictures. Everyone must have. Why then was I unprepared for the beauty of this region, for its variety of field and hill, forest, lake? . . . I remembered now that I had been told Wisconsin is a lovely state, but the telling had not prepared me.
—John Steinbeck, *Travels with Charley*

ALTHOUGH THIS LAND WAS OCCUPIED for thousands of years before becoming a state, the drawing of Wisconsin's state boundaries had a remarkable effect: it made people aware of who they were, where they were, and how they were different from people in other places, even people just over the border in Illinois, Minnesota, Iowa, and Michigan. Borders, however arbitrarily drawn, gave everyone who lived within them a common identity as Wisconsinites, even if they shared little else. And each of us who resides here has had a hand in creating what it means to live in this place.

As one view into the larger story of the United States, Wisconsin's history helps illuminate the history of the country. How one family in Racine dealt with fear of the atomic bomb reveals how national and even international events ripple down from the war room to the living room. The journals and accounts of French explorers and missionaries traveling through Wisconsin in the seventeenth century remind us that the future of the New World would be determined not on the East Coast but also in Wisconsin, where the competition for fur fueled tensions and the ambitions of colonial powers half a continent and an ocean away. In the late nineteenth and early twentieth centuries, Wisconsin's passage of workers' compensation legislation in response to nationwide labor issues and abuses set an example for the rest of the country. The state's history has followed the general patterns of the nation's, responding to the times and circumstances, but always with a particular flavor that is unique to the state and to the people who live here.

Wisconsin balances a zest for change with respect for history and tradition. For instance, despite a clear passion for reform—of schools, slavery, dairy farming, election laws, labor practices—Wisconsin has also preserved its constitution, with the exception of amendments, in the form in which it was written in 1847, making it the oldest state constitution outside of New England still in use. But it is Wisconsin's innovations, like unemployment insurance, commercial hydroelectric power, income tax, and Babcock's butterfat tester, that became models adopted across the nation.

More than the state's superlatives, however, the traits that define Wisconsin for its residents are rooted in the ordinary. For some, that lies in the sense of closeness to government: Wisconsinites can walk by and through the Capitol building almost any time. Others locate their Wisconsin-ness in an experience. Residents connect with the state's agricultural heritage at an abundance of high-quality farmers markets. Cross-country skiing across the snow dunes of a frozen lake on a cold, clear day epitomizes what it means to live in a place where winter is an elemental part of the hardiness of the Wisconsin character. And maybe what makes us Wisconsinites is our temperament: Wisconsin's people have a deserved reputation for being welcoming and genuinely friendly.

All of Wisconsin's characteristics—its variety of field and hill, forest and lake, its harsh winters and balmy summers, its ground-breaking inventions and its essential conviviality—are products of its past. And Wisconsinites' affection for their state and what makes it special will help to inform its future. When we talk about old times and family traditions, be it a relative lost to war, a first car, or recipes for Norwegian lefse or Hmong egg rolls, we are choosing and constructing the narratives that give our lives meaning and humanize a region on a map. History is created by the experiences of those who lived it. Wisconsin's story is still being written and rewritten, folding in the customs and traditions of Europeans, Indians, Hispanics, Asians, and all who call Wisconsin home.

ACKNOWLEDGMENTS

IT'S SOMETIMES DIFFICULT for me to remember a time when I didn't have Wisconsin history coursing through my brain. When the name Boscobel didn't immediately make me think of the Bible-distributing Gideons who got their start in a hotel room there, or when Ripon didn't call to mind first the utopian community of Ceresco and, later, the first meetings of the nascent Republican Party. And for this, I have the Wisconsin Historical Society to thank.

Barely three weeks after moving to Wisconsin for graduate school in 2002, I was approached by Michael Edmonds in the Society's reading room and asked if I wanted a job. Scarcely did I know that what began as a few hours in between coursework would become a calling of sorts—a calling to get to know my new home in a way that I never knew my home state of Washington. Despite loving history for most of my life, I had never taken much of an interest in the place where I was from. The history I loved (or so I thought) was far away, on the east coast. Working with Michael at the Wisconsin Historical Society changed all of that for me.

Much of the research for this book was done while working with Michael on the online state history collection "Turning Points in Wisconsin History" and on the *Dictionary of Wisconsin History*. I thank him for his unflagging support, trust, and willingness to take a chance on someone whose only immediately visible skill was to be in the right place at the right time.

Thanks also to the generations of librarians and archivists at the Wisconsin Historical Society who have had the good sense to collect the obscure, offbeat, as well as the essential records of Wisconsin's past. And to the Wisconsin Historical Society Press for their enthusiasm for the project and to my editor Michelle Wildgen for her skill and encouragement.

My parents, Bill and Karin, have listened to me rant and rave about this or that for decades now, and I thank them for continuing to listen and for offering their support. The same goes for many of my beleaguered and wonderful friends, especially Erica Davis, Hillary Jensen, Nicole Miller, Natasha Sattin, Amanda Raster, Mary Ellen Gabriel, Sara Gibbs, and Laura Kearney.

And finally to Matt Jensen, without whose love, patience, and good humor my life would be far less rich. He sat across from me in coffee shops as I wrote much of this book, sensitive to the travails of writing as I, hands poised over my laptop, stared blankly at the ceiling. His sympathetic but incisive criticism and suggestions made this a much better history.

ESSAY ON SOURCES
AND SUGGESTIONS FOR FURTHER READING

THIS ESSAY IS LIMITED TO THE TOPICS covered in this book. Even within these limits, it focuses for the most part on items I found most reliable, useful, and representative. While my suggestions are divided by chapters, many of the items pertain to issues in multiple chapters.

The best general history of Wisconsin with information on many of the issues and topics discussed in this book can be found in the daunting but invaluable six-volume *History of Wisconsin* series published by the State Historical Society. Many of the best articles on Wisconsin history topics have been published in the *Wisconsin Magazine of History*, access to which is now much easier thanks to the digitized archives of every issue dating back to its beginning in 1917 at www.wisconsinhistory.org/wmh. The *Wisconsin Blue Book*, a biennial publication of the state's Legislative Reference Bureau, also contains numerous historical essays and invaluable economic, political, and demographic information. Another excellent source of secondary and primary sources on Wisconsin history, including many of the documents referenced here, can be found in the Wisconsin Historical Society's digital collection "Turning Points in Wisconsin History" at www.wisconsinhistory.org/turningpoints. For more primary and secondary sources on hundreds of Wisconsin history topics, see Barbara Dotts Paul and Justus F. Paul's *Wisconsin History: An Annotated Bibliography* (Westport, CT: Greenwood Press, 1999).

GEOGRAPHY OF PLACE

A number of books explore Wisconsin's physical environment. Standard works include: *Wisconsin's Past and Present: A Historical Atlas* by The Wisconsin Cartographers' Guild (Madison: University of Wisconsin Press, 1998); and *The Physical Geography of Wisconsin* by Lawrence Martin (Madison: University of Wisconsin Press, 1916; 3rd edition, 1965). See also Marvin W. Burley, "The Climate of Wisconsin," in the *Wisconsin Blue Book, 1964*, pg. 143–148, and Gwen Schultz, *Wisconsin's Foundations: A Review of the State's Geology and Its Influence on Geography and Human Activity* (Madison: UW Cooperative Extension Service, 1986). The most useful guide to locating places in the physical and built environments is Arthur H. Robinson and Jerry B. Culver, eds., *The Atlas of Wisconsin: General Maps and Gazetteer* (Madison: University of Wisconsin Press, 1974).

One of the earliest accounts of Wisconsin's physical environment can be found in the colorful and opinionated account of British geologist George W. Featherstonhaugh, *A Canoe Voyage up the Minnay Sotor; with an Account of the Lead and Copper Deposits in Wisconsin* . . . (London: R. Bentley, 1847). Featherstonhaugh's earlier account, *Report of a Geological Reconnaissance Made in 1835 from the Seat of Government, by the way of Green Bay and the Wisconsin Territory to the Coteau de Prairie, an Elevated Ridge Dividing the Missouri from the St. Peter's River* (Washington, D.C.: Gales and Seaton, 1836) is primarily a geological account of Wisconsin.

Patty Loew's classic *Indian Nations of Wisconsin: Histories of Endurance and Renewal* (Madison: Wisconsin Historical Society Press, 2001) is an indispensable guide to Wisconsin's Native peoples. There are several important early studies of Wisconsin Indians. One of the earliest archaeological reports on the copper culture and ancient copper mining by Indians in the Lake Superior area comes from Charles Whittlesey in "Ancient Mining on the Shores of Lake Superior" (Washington, D.C.: Smithsonian Institution, 1863; Smithsonian Contributions to Knowledge, no. 155). The first careful investigation of Wisconsin mounds was published in 1838 by Richard C. Taylor, "Notes Respecting Certain Indian Mounds and Earthworks, in the form of Animal Effigies, Chiefly in the Wisconsin Territory, U.S.," *American Journal of Science and Arts* XXXIV (July 1838): 88–104. Increase Lapham's scholarly book on effigy mounds is filled with maps, lithographs, and careful descriptions still useful today: *The Antiquities of Wisconsin* (Washington, D.C.: Smithsonian Institution, 1855).

The best book on Wisconsin's Indian mounds is *Indian Mounds of Wisconsin* by Robert A. Birmingham and Leslie E. Eisenberg (Madison: University of Wisconsin Press, 2000). An excellent introduction and examination of the Mississippian community can be found in Robert A. Birmingham and Lynne G. Goldstein's *Aztalan: Mysteries of an Ancient Indian Town* (Madison: Wisconsin Historical Society Press, 2006).

FORTUNES MADE OF FUR

Between 1855 and 1915, the Wisconsin Historical Society published a series of volumes comprised of historical documents relating to state history called the *Wisconsin Historical Collections* (Madison: State Historical Society of Wisconsin). Volumes 11 and 16 are especially useful for documents on the first Europeans in Wisconsin, and volumes 16 through 19 contain the most information on the French fur trade. Some of the documents published in the *Wisconsin Historical Collections* come from the *Jesuit Relations*, a series of reports from Jesuit missions in New France published annually in Paris between 1632 and 1673. The reports were collected and published as *The Jesuit Relations and Allied Documents* by Reuben Gold Thwaites (Cleveland: The Burrows Brothers, 1898).

Early Europeans left a wide range of journals, diaries, letters, and other accounts of their explorations and experiences in Wisconsin. The first French explorers to visit Wisconsin after Nicolet were Pierre-Esprit Radisson and his brother-in-law Médard Chouart Des Groseilliers. Radisson's trips have been collected in *Voyages of*

Peter Esprit Radisson, Being an Account of his Travels and Experiences among the North American Indians, from 1652 to 1684, ed. Gideon D. Scull (Boston: Prince Society, 1885). Father Marquette's journal of his Mississippi voyage with Louis Joliet can be found in "The Mississippi Voyage of Jolliet and Marquette" in Louise P. Kellogg, ed., *Early Narratives of the Northwest, 1634–1699* (New York: Charles Scribner's Sons, 1917): 221–258. Other exploration narratives of note: Jean Claude Allouez, "Father Allouez's Journey to Lake Superior, 1665–1667" in Louise P. Kellogg, ed., *Early Narratives of the Northwest, 1634–1699* (New York: Charles Scribner's Sons, 1917): 93–138; Barthelemy Vimont, "Journey of Jean Nicolet, 1634" in Louise P. Kellogg, ed., *Early Narratives of the Northwest, 1634–1699* (New York: Charles Scribner's Sons, 1917): 9–16; and Nicolas Perrot, "Adventures of Nicolas Perrot, 1665–1670" in Louise P. Kellogg, ed., *Early Narratives of the Northwest, 1634–1699* (New York: Charles Scribner's Sons, 1917): 67–92. Two Indian accounts of first contact with Europeans can be found in Paul Radin, "How the Winnebago First Came into Contact with the French and the Origin of the Decora Family," in *The Winnebago Tribe* (Washington, D.C.: U.S. Government Printing Office, 1923): 65–69; and in Walter James Hoffman, "The First Meeting of the Menomini and the Whites" in *The Menomini Indians* (Washington, D.C.: U.S. Government Printing Office, 1896): 214–216.

For contemporary accounts of the fur trade, see: Louis Armand de Lom d'Arce, Baron de Lahontan, *New Voyages to North America* (London, 1703); Pierre Francois Xavier de Charlevoix "Letter XX [on his 1721 visit to Wisconsin]" in *Journal of a Voyage to North-America* (London, 1761); Augustin Grignon, "Seventy-two Years' Recollections of Wisconsin" in *Wisconsin Historical Collections* 3 (Madison: State Historical Society of Wisconsin, 1857): 194–295; and Antoine Grignon, "Recollections of Antoine Grignon," *Proceedings of the State Historical Society at its 61st Annual Meeting Held Oct. 22 and Dec. 19, 1913* (Madison, 1914): 110–136.

The gathering of wild rice was much remarked upon by early explorers. The most thorough and comprehensive description of wild rice and its importance to Native American peoples was published by Albert Ernest Jenks, quoting liberally from Indian informants as well as three centuries of travel narratives: *The Wild Rice Gatherers of the Upper Lakes: A Study of American Primitive Economics* (Washington, D.C.: U.S. Government Printing Office, 1900).

FROM TERRITORY TO STATEHOOD

The Northwest Ordinance set the guidelines for how new lands, including Wisconsin, should be surveyed. The text of the ordinance, known as "An Ordinance for the Government of the Territory of the United States Northwest of the River Ohio," is available in full on the website of the National Archives and Records Administration at www.ourdocuments.gov. The field notes and plats of Wisconsin drawn by General Land Office surveyors are available online from the University of Wisconsin-Madison Digital Collections Center at libtext.library.wisc.edu/SurveyNotes.

Much has been written on the Black Hawk War, particularly contemporary accounts. Black Hawk's own autobiography, available in many places online, is a good place to start: *Autobiography of Ma Ka Tai Kia Kiak, or Black Hawk . . .* (Rock Island, IL, 1833). Other good recountings through both Indian and white eyes are: Mauchhewemahnigo (Walking Cloud), "Narrative of Walking Cloud," *Wisconsin Historical Collections* 13 (Madison: State Historical Society of Wisconsin, 1895): 463–467; Joseph Dickson, "Personal Narrative of the Black Hawk War, 1855," in *Wisconsin Historical Collections* 5 (Madison: State Historical Society of Wisconsin, 1868): 315–320; Perry A. Armstrong, *The Sauks and the Black Hawk War, with Biographical Sketches, Etc.* (Springfield, IL: H. W. Rokker, 1887); and collected reminiscences from Iowa settlers, "Reminiscences of Black Hawk, by People who Knew him," *Burlington (IA) Hawk-Eye*, (24 March 1907). The geography of the war and Black Hawk's retreat through Wisconsin is conveniently provided by William Thomas Hagan in *Black Hawk's Route through Wisconsin: Report of an Inves-*

tigation Made by Authority of the Legislature of Wisconsin (Madison: State Historical Society of Wisconsin, 1949).

Many early settlers wrote memoirs touching on their years in early Wisconsin. One of the most popular is Juliette Kinzie's *Waubun, the Early Days of the Northwest* (New York: Derby & Jackson, 1856) about her life at Fort Winnebago, 1829–34, where her husband served as U.S. Indian sub-agent. See also Rasmus B. Anderson's *Life Story of Rasmus B. Anderson* (Madison, 1915); William W. Bartlett's *History, Tradition and Adventure in the Chippewa Valley* (Chippewa Falls, WI: The Chippewa Printery, 1929); and Elizabeth T. Baird, "Reminiscences of Life in Territorial Wisconsin," *Wisconsin Historical Collections* 15 (Madison: State Historical Society of Wisconsin, 1900): 205–263.

The texts of all Indian treaties with Wisconsin Indians can be found in volume two of the seven-volume *Indian Affairs: Laws and Treaties* by Charles J. Kappler, (Washington, D.C.: U.S. Department of the Interior, 1904–1979). Maps and tables showing the boundaries of all lands ceded by Indian nations to the U.S. government can be found in "Indian Land Cessions in the United States, 1784–1894," House Document No. 736, 56th Congress, 1st Session (United States Serial Set Number 4015).

Creating Wisconsin's state constitution was a long, difficult process. Joseph A. Ranney provides an excellent overview in "Wisconsin's Legal History: The Making of the Wisconsin Constitution," in the *Wisconsin Lawyer* (Madison: State Bar of Wisconsin), online at www.wisbar.org. Transcripts of the debates over the provisions of the first and second Constitutions, including women's rights and allowing immigrants to vote, can be found in *Wisconsin Historical Collections* volumes 27 and 28 (Madison: State Historical Society of Wisconsin, 1919 and 1920).

CALLING WISCONSIN HOME

Many immigrant groups came to call Wisconsin home in the nineteenth century and there are literally hundreds of published works on Wisconsin's ethnic history. The most detailed portraits of these people can be found in the ever-expanding *People of Wisconsin* series from the Wisconsin Historical Society Press. Books in the series to date: *Danes in Wisconsin, Irish in Wisconsin, Germans in Wisconsin, Norwegians in Wisconsin, Swedes in Wisconsin, Swiss in Wisconsin, Welsh in Wisconsin,* and *Finns in Wisconsin.* Volumes 14 and 15 of the *Wisconsin Historical Collections* (Madison: State Historical Society of Wisconsin, 1898 and 1900) include many recollections of coming to and settling in Wisconsin. Women's settlement experiences, in particular, are described by Joan M. Jensen in *Calling This Place Home: Women on the Wisconsin Frontier, 1850–1925* (St. Paul: Minnesota Historical Society Press, 2006).

Immigrant handbooks also offer detailed information on Wisconsin, or at least the perception the author wanted immigrants to have of the state. These include: Samuel Freeman, *The Emigrant's Hand Book, and Guide to Wisconsin: Comprising Information Respecting Agricultural and Manufacturing Employment, Wages, Climate, Population &c; Sketch of Milwaukee . . .* (Milwaukee: Sentinel and Gazette Power Press Print, 1851); and William Arnon Henry, *Northern Wisconsin, A Hand-Book for the Homeseeker* (Madison: Democrat printing company, state printer, 1896).

Works on Wisconsin's waterways are numerous. Giacomo Costantino Beltrami was aboard the first steamboat to travel the upper Mississippi, a trip he described in his travel narrative, *Pilgrimage in Europe and America, Leading to the Discovery of the Sources of the Mississippi and Bloody River: With a Description of the Whole Course of the Former, and of the Ohio . . .* (London: Hunt, 1828), vol. 2: 126–197. Steamboat pilot George Byron Merrick recalls his nine colorful years as a steamboat pilot in *Old Times on the Upper Mississippi: The Recollections of a Steamboat Pilot from 1854 to 1863* (Cleveland: A. H. Clark Co., 1909). The proposal to unite Lake Michigan with the Rock River gets a full treatment by Increase Lapham in *A Documentary History of the Milwaukee and Rock River Canal, Compiled and Published by Order of the Board of Directors of the Milwaukee and Rock River*

Canal Company (Milwaukee: Office of the Advertiser, 1840). John Disturnell published an exhaustive and informative guide to the resources and travel possibilities of the Great Lakes and regional rivers in 1874: *Sailing on the Great Lakes and Rivers of America* (Philadelphia: J. Disturnell, 1874).

LEAD AND LUMBER

Mining of lead in southwestern Wisconsin can be traced back to at least 1670. An overview can be found in Carol March McLernon, *Lead-Mining Towns of Southwest Wisconsin* (Charleston, SC: Arcadia Publishing, 2008). "Notes on Early Lead Mining in the Fever (or Galena) River Region" by Reuben Gold Thwaites, *Wisconsin Historical Collections* 13 (Madison: State Historical Society of Wisconsin, 1895): 271–292, is a chronological review of quotes and primary sources describing lead mining before the big boom of the 1830s. For contemporary accounts of life in the lead region, see: Moses Meeker, "Early History of the Lead Region of Wisconsin," *Wisconsin Historical Collections* 6 (Madison: State Historical Society of Wisconsin, 1872): 271–296; Theodore Rodolf, "Pioneering in the Wisconsin Lead Region," *Wisconsin Historical Collections* 15 (Madison: State Historical Society of Wisconsin, 1898): 338–389; and Spoon DeKaury, "Narrative of Spoon Decorah," *Wisconsin Historical Collections* 13 (Madison: State Historical Society of Wisconsin, 1895): 448–462. Contemporary accounts of northern mining can be found in John R. St. John, *A True Description of the Lake Superior Country* (New York: W. H. Graham, 1846).

The history of logging and lumbering in Wisconsin has been extensively studied by members of the Forest History Association of Wisconsin. Their scholarship, covering everything from school forests and logging on Indian reservations to forest fire protection, is published annually in the *Proceedings of the Forest History Association* (Wausau, WI: The Association). Mark Wyman's *The Wisconsin Frontier: A History of the Trans-Appalachian Frontier* (Bloomington:

Indiana University Press, 1998) covers many areas of state history through the nineteenth century but extensively describes the extraction of resources including lumber. The devastation wrought by lumbering incited Increase Lapham to write the first conservation plea in 1867: *Report on the Disastrous Effects of the Destruction of Forest Trees, Now Going on so Rapidly in the State of Wisconsin* (Madison: Atwood & Rublee, 1867). Lumberjack life is amusingly recalled by Thomas McBean in "The Lumber Camps of Long Ago: A Chippewa Pioneer Writes Interestingly of the Logging Camps on the Chippewa River in the Long Ago," *Chippewa Falls Independent* (14 January 1915).

Wisconsin's cutover has attracted more than its share of scholars; among them are Robert J. Gough, *Farming the Cutover: A Social History of Northern Wisconsin, 1900–1940* (Lawrence: University of Kansas Press, 1997); and Vernon R. Carstensen, *Farms or Forests: Evolution of a State Land Policy for Northern Wisconsin, 1850–1932* (Madison: University of Wisconsin, College of Agriculture, 1958; reprinted New York, 1979). See also "Made-to-Order Farms: Benjamin Faast's Vision for Northern Wisconsin" by Erika Janik in the *Wisconsin Magazine of History* 90 (Summer 2007): 40–49 for more on development schemes for the cutover.

SOCIAL AND MORAL IMPROVEMENT

Schools were some of the first and most important social institutions established in Wisconsin. Information on Wisconsin's first professional teacher, Electa Quinney, is limited to a few articles, including "The First Wisconsin Teacher," *Wisconsin Journal of Education*, new series, vol. 18 (Madison, 1888): 493–494. Among other items relating to the development of educational institutions, including reminiscences from teachers, are: "Guest Tells of Old Days in Milwaukee: Mrs. Samuel Wells Buck Revives Student Memories of Female College 60 Years Ago," *Milwaukee Journal* (14 August 1927); "The First Teacher of Domestic Science," *Milwaukee Journal* (9 July

1929); Mary D. Bradford, *Memoirs of Mary D. Bradford* . . . (Evansville, WI: The Antes Press, 1932); and Helen Maria Remington Olin, *The Women of a State University: An Illustration of the Working of Coeducation in the Middle West* (New York: G. P. Putnam's Sons, 1909). Additionally, the effects of and opposition to the Bennett Law are discussed in William F. Whyte, "The Bennett Law Campaign in Wisconsin," *Wisconsin Magazine of History* 10 (June 1927): 363–390.

A fair amount of research has been done on Indian education in recent decades. One of the better histories covering the broad spectrum of Indian experiences in missionary, government, and tribal boarding and day schools is provided by Jon Reyhner and Jeanne Eder in *American Indian Education: A History* (Norman: University of Oklahoma Press, 2004). The sometimes dreadful conditions of Indian schools were not unknown, and in the 1830s missionary Richard F. Cadle defended his American-style school for Indian children in "Documents relating to the Episcopal Church and Mission in Green Bay, 1825–41: Conditions of Admission and Survey of Schools," *Wisconsin Historical Collections* 14 (Madison: State Historical Society of Wisconsin, 1898): 450–476. Father Samuel C. Mazzuchelli's memoirs describe building churches, organizing schools, and preaching through the upper Great Lakes to Indians and immigrants: *Memoirs of a Missionary Apostolic* . . . (Chicago: W. F. Hall, 1915).

The religious development of Wisconsin is discussed in Rembert G. Weakland, "The Religious Landscape of Wisconsin: From Steeples to the Unknown," *Wisconsin Academy Review* (Winter 1999–2000): 37–39; Brian W. Beltman, "Rural Church Reform in Wisconsin During the Progressive Era," *Wisconsin Magazine of History* 60 (Autumn 1976): 2–24; and Thomas S. Johnson, "Moses Ordway, Pioneer Presbyterian Missionary," *Wisconsin Magazine of History* 2 (March 1919): 265–273.

Lizzie Black Kander (often called the Jane Addams of Wisconsin) and her Milwaukee settlement house are well covered by Angela Fritz, "Lizzie Black Kander and Culinary Reform in Milwaukee, 1880–1920," *Wisconsin Magazine of History* 87 (Spring 2004): 36–49, and Bob Kann in the children's book *A Recipe for Success: Lizzie Kander and Her Cookbook* (Madison: Wisconsin Historical Society Press, 2007).

One of the most complete and readable portraits of Wisconsin's labor history is anthologized by Darryl Holter in *Workers and Unions in Wisconsin: A Labor History Anthology* (Madison: Wisconsin Historical Society Press, 2000). John R. Commons, best known today as the founder of labor history, played an influential role in passing some of the most important social reforms enacted on the state and national level. His four-volume *History of Labour in the United States* (New York, 1918–1935) is a comprehensive examination of labor history nationally. Additionally, Commons's autobiography offers many insights and anecdotes on the state Industrial Commission and labor legislation: John R. Commons, *Myself* (New York: The Macmillan Co., 1934).

CIVIL WAR WISCONSIN

There may be no aspect of American history more documented than the Civil War. Among the best on Wisconsin are Stephen E. Ambrose, *Wisconsin Boy in Dixie: Civil War Letters of James K. Newton* (Madison: University of Wisconsin Press, 1995); Richard H. Zeitlin, *Old Abe the War Eagle: A True Story of the Civil War and Reconstruction* (Madison: State Historical Society of Wisconsin, 1986); and Frank Klement, *Wisconsin in the Civil War: The Home Front and The Battle Front, 1861–1865* (Madison: State Historical Society of Wisconsin, 1963). Women's experiences during the war get their own treatment in Ethel Alice Hurn, *Wisconsin Women in the War Between the States* (Wisconsin History Commission, 1911). Researching Civil War history is made much easier by Brett Barker in *Exploring Civil War Wisconsin: A Survival Guide for Researchers* (Madison: Wisconsin Historical Society Press, 2003), as well as through first person narrative accounts in "Wisconsin Goes to War: Our Civil War Experience," available online from the University of Wisconsin Digital Collections at http://digital

.library.wisc.edu/1711.dl/WI.WIWar. Private Reuben Sweet of She-boygan describes his wartime experiences, including accounts of bat-tles and skirmishes from Tennessee to Atlanta, in his "Civil War Diary of Reuben Sweet," *Antigo Daily Journal* (9 March 1939).

The literature on slavery and abolitionism in Wisconsin is much smaller than that on the war. The experiences of those who helped fugitive slaves escape were collected by J. N. Davidson in *Negro Slavery in Wisconsin and the Underground Railroad* (Milwaukee: Parkman Club, 1897). The most famous slave to pass through Wisconsin, Joshua Glover, whose escape led to Wisconsin's nullification of the federal fugitive slave law, is described by Henry E. Legler, "Rescue of Joshua Glover, a Runaway Slave," in *Leading Events of Wisconsin History* (Milwaukee: Sentinel, 1898), and more recently in Ruby West Jackson and Walter T. McDonald, *Finding Freedom: The Untold Story of Joshua Glover, Runaway Slave* (Madison: Wisconsin Historical Society Press, 2007). The children's book *Caroline Quarlls and the Underground Railroad* by Julia Pferdehirt (Madison: Wisconsin Historical Society Press, 2008) is a solid introduction to the life of the first known slave to escape to freedom through Wisconsin.

BECOMING AMERICA'S DAIRYLAND

Two of the best general surveys of Wisconsin agriculture end in the 1920s: Joseph Schafer, *A History of Agriculture in Wisconsin* (Madison: State Historical Society of Wisconsin, 1922), and Eric E. Lampard, *The Rise of the Dairy Industry in Wisconsin: A Study in Agricultural Change, 1820–1920* (Madison: State Historical Society of Wisconsin, 1963).

Agriculture generates more than its share of statistics, the most useful of which is the census of agriculture published at five-year intervals by the U.S. Census Bureau. Also useful is the statistical summary of Wisconsin's dairying industry from 1860–1930, produced by Walter H. Ebling and called "Wisconsin Dairying" (Madison: Wisconsin Crop and Livestock Reporting Service, 1931).

Farm journals are a rich source of technical as well as personal information on farming. Among them are the *Wisconsin Agriculturalist* (previously known as the *Wisconsin Agriculturalist and Farmer*), *Hoard's Dairyman*, and *Badger Farm Bureau News*.

The transition from wheat to dairy farming is described by Norman K. Risjord in "From the Plow to the Cow: William D. Hoard and America's Dairyland," *Wisconsin Magazine of History* 88 (Spring 2005): 40–49, and Wilbur Stiles in "Lake Mills: A Dairying Pioneer," *Wisconsin Magazine of History* 24 (Summer 1941): 446–452.

There are only a few books on William Dempster Hoard, the tireless promoter of Wisconsin's move toward dairy farming: George William Rankin, *William Dempster Hoard* (Fort Atkinson, WI: W. D. Hoard & Sons Co., 1925); *William Dempster Hoard: A Builder of American Dairying* (Madison: Agricultural Extension Service, 1932); and Loren H. Osman, *W. D. Hoard: A Man for His Time* (Fort Atkinson, WI: W. D. Hoard, 1985).

Wisconsin's cheese industry has attracted a large number of guides, with a little history thrown in, to the state's cheeses, including: Martin Hinz and Pam Percy, *Wisconsin Cheese: A Cookbook and Guide to the Cheeses of Wisconsin* (Guilford, CT: Globe Pequot, 2008), and Jerry Apps, *Cheese: The Making of a Wisconsin Tradition* (Madison: University of Wisconsin Press, 2004). To understand the development of the cheese industry in Wisconsin from its beginnings through 1950, see Loyal Durand Jr., "The Cheese Manufacturing Regions of Wisconsin, 1850–1950," *Transactions of the Wisconsin Academy of Sciences, Arts and Letters* (1953): 109–130.

Wisconsin's other agricultural products have received far less historical attention than dairying. Vegetable growing and canning has received scant attention outside of industry and government reports save for Frederick Stare, "Wisconsin's Canning Industry, Past and Present," *Wisconsin Magazine of History* 36 (Autumn 1952): 34–38. The early days of cranberry cultivation are told in "Cranberries. A Description of Great Marshes," *Milwaukee Commercial Times* (12 April 1875). The hop craze, while brief, had a big impact on Sauk

County, as told by John Rooney in "Hop Culture in Days Long Past," *Baraboo News* (26 October 1911).

The best article on the development of meatpacking is Paul E. Geib, "Everything But the Squeal: The Milwaukee Stockyards and Meat-packing Industry, 1840–1930," *Wisconsin Magazine of History* 78 (Autumn 1994): 2–23.

MANUFACTURING THE FUTURE

Industrial statistics stream constantly from the various levels of government, universities, private organizations, and groups ranging from regional planning commissions to industrial development committees, as well as from the companies themselves. Although useful, they can be dry reading. An early but still helpful introduction to the rise of manufacturing is J. H. H. Alexander, "A Short Industrial History of Wisconsin," *Wisconsin Blue Book, 1929*: 31–49. Insight into Wisconsin's business climate can be found in Warren J. Samuels, "An Overview of the Relationship of Wisconsin State Government to Business," *Wisconsin Blue Book, 1956*: 71–82. Focused only on Milwaukee, W. W. Coleman's *Milwaukee Illustrated: Its Trade, Commerce, Manufacturing, Interests, and Advantages as a Residence City* (Milwaukee: W. W. Coleman, 1877) provides an extended and somewhat opinionated description of the city's major industries and commercial operations.

Local and regional business economies developed throughout the state. The best place to start is Philip Sundal and Richard Kotenbeutel, *Geography of Wisconsin Manufacturing* (Madison: Department of Local Affairs and Development, Division of Economic Development, 4th ed. 1970). To learn more about the heavily industrialized southeastern counties, consult *The Economy of Southeastern Wisconsin*, Southeastern Wisconsin Regional Planning Commission, *Planning Report, no. 3* (Waukesha, WI, 1963).

For information on specific companies and their products, promotional and marketing literature produced by the companies themselves can often be a good place to start. The Edward P. Allis Company published a wide range of booklets and catalogues, including *Edward P. Allis and Company Reliance Works: Illustrated Catalogue of Roller Mills and other Special Machinery* (Milwaukee: Cramer, Aikens, Engravers and Printers, 1888). For its sixtieth anniversary, the Aluminum Manufacturing Company produced a company history that also tells the story of the aluminum industry in Manitowoc: "Mixing Bowl 60th Anniversary edition, 1895–1955, and related Mirro Aluminum materials," Aluminum Manufacturing Company (July 1955).

THE SPORTING LIFE

As time for and the number of leisure and recreational opportunities has increased, so too has the literature on the topic. The best introduction to the topic is Foster Rhea Dulles, *America Learns to Play: A History of Popular Recreation, 1607–1940* (New York: D. Appleton-Century Company, 1940). The idea of leisure time and how attitudes toward it have developed and changed are explored in Margaret Mead, "The Pattern of Leisure in Contemporary American Culture," in *The Annals of the American Academy of Political and Social Science* 313 (September 1957): 11–15; David Riesman, "Some Observations on Changes in Leisure Attitudes," in *Antioch Review* 12 (December 1952): 417–436; and David Riesman and Reuel Denney, "Football in America: A Study in Culture Diffusion," in *American Quarterly* 3 (Winter 1951): 309–325.

Wisconsin's sports history has been written largely by journalists, so the best place to begin for all but the best known Wisconsin teams is the sports section of local papers. The Oshkosh *Daily Northwestern*, for example, published a ten-part series on the Oshkosh All-Stars of the National Professional Basketball League from January 6 through January 17, 1979.

On the Green Bay Packers, see Michael O'Brien's *Vince: A Personal Biography of Vince Lombardi* (New York: Morrow, 1987); David Maraniss, *When Pride Still Mattered: A Life of Vince Lombardi* (New York:

Simon & Schuster, 2nd ed. 1999); and David Zimmerman, *Lambeau: The Man Behind the Mystique* (Hales Corners, WI: Eagle Books, 2003).

The Milwaukee Braves have received most of the attention paid to baseball history in Wisconsin. The best book on the team's rise and fall is William Povletich's *Milwaukee Braves: Heroes and Heartbreak* (Madison: Wisconsin Historical Society Press, 2009). See also Povletich's article on the Braves' 1957 championship season, "When the Braves of Bushville Ruled Baseball: Celebrating Andy Pafko and the 1957 Milwaukee Braves," *Wisconsin Magazine of History* 90 (Summer 2007): 2–14. On professional baseball prior to the Braves, see Harry H. Anderson, "The Ancient Origins of Baseball in Milwaukee," in *Milwaukee History* 6 (Summer 1983): 42–57. For the story of the original Milwaukee Brewers, who spent fifty-one seasons as part of the American Association, see Rex Hamann and Bob Koehler, *American Association Milwaukee Brewers* (Charleston, SC: Arcadia, 2004). The coming of the professional league Brewers and their 1982 American League Pennant win is recounted in Robert De Broux's "The 1982 Brewers Dared Wisconsin Fans to Fall in Love Again," *Wisconsin Magazine of History* 90 (Summer 2007): 16–21. Baseball was also popular among the Indians, excellently recounted by Patty Loew in "Tinker to Evers to Chief: Baseball from Indian Country," *Wisconsin Magazine of History* 87 (Spring 2004): 2–13.

The best and most complete story of the sport that made Wisconsin famous is told by Doug Schmidt in *They Came to Bowl: How Milwaukee Became America's Tenpin Capital* (Madison: Wisconsin Historical Society Press, 2007).

Though not about Wisconsin specifically, the most complete history of curling can be found in Doug Clark's *The Roaring Game: A Sweeping Saga of Curling* (Toronto: Key Porter Books, 2008).

PROGRESSIVE POLITICS

The Progressive Era and its major figures have not lacked for historical scholarship. Overviews of the time period and its major changes and innovations can be found in Steven J. Diner's *A Very Different Age: Americans of the Progressive Era* (New York: Hill and Wang, 1998); Page Smith, *America Enters the World: A People's History of the Progressive Era and World War I* (New York: McGraw-Hill, 1985); Michael McGerr, *A Fierce Discontent: The Rise and Fall of the Progressive Movement in America, 1870–1920* (Oxford: Oxford University Press, 2005); and of course, John D. Buenker's *The History of Wisconsin vol. 4: The Progressive Era, 1893–1914* (Madison: Wisconsin Historical Society Press, 1998).

Many biographies have been written on Robert M. La Follette but the best is Nancy C. Unger's *Fighting Bob La Follette: The Righteous Reformer* (Madison: Wisconsin Historical Society Press, pbk. ed. 2008). Important insights into La Follette's life and mind can be found in his *Autobiography: A Personal Narrative of Political Experiences* (Madison: R. M. La Follette Co., 1913). Valuable explorations of the other La Follettes include Lucy Freeman's *Belle: The Biography of Belle Case La Follette* (New York: Beaufort Books, 1986); Patrick J. Maney, *Young Bob: A Biography of Robert M. La Follette, Jr.* (Madison: Wisconsin Historical Society Press, 2nd ed. 2002); and Jonathan Kasparek, *Fighting Son: A Biography of Philip F. La Follette* (Madison: Wisconsin Historical Society Press, 2006).

Genevieve McBride has written two books on Wisconsin women's history and fight for rights: *Women's Wisconsin: From Native Matriarchies to the New Millennium* (Madison: Wisconsin Historical Society Press, 2005) and *On Wisconsin Women: Working for Their Rights from Settlement to Suffrage* (Madison: University of Wisconsin Press, 1993). See also James Howell Smith's article on peace activist and suffragette "Mrs. Ben Hooper of Oshkosh: Peace Worker and Politician," *Wisconsin Magazine of History* 46 (Winter 1962–63): 124–135.

WORLD WAR I

Wisconsin's role in the first world war has been far less documented than its part in the second world war. Though it claims not to be a comprehensive history of the war, Fred Holmes's *Wisconsin's War Record* (Madison: Capital Historical Publishing Co., 1919) provides substantial information about the draft, soldiers, women, war organizations, and the activities of assorted government agencies. Women's contributions to the war effort (chapter XXVII focuses on Wisconsin in particular) are summarized in Ida Clyde Gallagher Clarke's *American Women and the World War* (New York: D. Appleton and Company, 1918).

The letters, journals, and diaries of Wisconsin soldiers provide firsthand accounts of wartime experiences: Ira Berlin, ed., "A Wisconsinite in World War I: Reminiscences of Edmund P. Arpin, Jr. (Part II: Action)," *Wisconsin Magazine of History* 51 (Winter 1967–1968): 124–138; Sean Patrick Adams and Michael E. Stevens, eds., "'The Padre at the Front': The World War I Letters of Chaplain Walter Beaudette," *Wisconsin Magazine of History* 79 (Spring 1996): 204–228; Joe Michael Feist, ed., "A Wisconsin Man in the Russian Railway Service Corps: Letters of Fayette W. Keeler, 1918–1919," *Wisconsin Magazine of History* 62 (Spring 1979): 217–244; George C. Brown, ed., "With the Ambulance Service in France: The Wartime Letters of William Gorham Rice, Jr." *Wisconsin Magazine of History* 64 (Summer 1981): 278–293; and Arnold Runde and Fritz Schmidt "Letters from the Boys," *Neenah Daily Times* (8 January 1918). The Wisconsin Veterans Museum and the University of Wisconsin-Milwaukee produced an online collection of letters from Wisconsin soldiers and their families representing all branches of services and all ranks of personnel: "Wisconsin War Letters: World War I," online at www.uwm.edu/Library/arch/Warletters/wwi/WWI.htm.

Home front activities, events, and opinions, particularly toward German Americans, are richly described in several articles: David Zonderman, "Over Here: The Wisconsin Homefront During World War I," *Wisconsin Magazine of History* 77 (Summer 1994): 295–300; Lorin Lee Cary, "The Wisconsin Loyalty Legion, 1917–1918," *Wisconsin Magazine of History* 53 (Autumn 1969): 33–50; Karen Falk, "Public Opinion in Wisconsin during World War I," *Wisconsin Magazine of*

History 25 (June 1942): 389–407; Carl Wittke, "American Germans in Two World Wars," *Wisconsin Magazine of History* 27 (September 1943): 6–16; Wayne A. Wiegand, "In Service to the State: Wisconsin Public Libraries During World War I," *Wisconsin Magazine of History* 72 (Spring 1989): 199–224; and Walter I. Trattner, "Julia Grace Wales and the Wisconsin Plan for Peace," *Wisconsin Magazine of History* 44 (Spring 1961): 203–213.

CHANGING HABITS OF CONSUMPTION

Titles dealing specifically with electric power and the automobile industry in Wisconsin have yet to be written, though there are many good books on the spread of both nationally.

On electricity generally, see Robert Silverberg's *Light for the World: Edison and the Power Industry* (Princeton, NJ: Van Nostrand, 1967), and Jill Jonnes, *Empires of Light: Edison, Tesla, Westinghouse, and the Race to Electrify the World* (New York: Random House, 2003); on rural electrification specifically, see Michael J. Goc's *Where the Waters Flow: A Half Century of Regional Development, 1941–1991* (Friendship, WI: New Past Press, 1991), and Clayton D. Brown, *Electricity for Rural America: The Fight for the REA* (Westport, CT: Greenwood Press, 1980). The story of the nation's first commercial light and power plant in Appleton is told by David Lowater in "First Light and Power Plant Was Built in Wisconsin," *Wisconsin State Journal* (14 December 1924) and Frank L. Holmes, "Badger City Home of First Electric Plant in America," *Milwaukee Sentinel* (20 November 1921).

For general automobile history, see Frank Coffey, *America on Wheels: The First 100 Years: 1896–1996* (Los Angeles: General Publishing Group, 1998) for a social and industrial history of cars. A corollary to automobiles, gas stations changed the American landscape, a history richly documented for Wisconsin by Jim Draeger and Mark Speltz in *Fill 'er Up: The Glory Days of Wisconsin Gas Stations* (Madison: Wisconsin Historical Society Press, 2008). The origins of the Harley-Davidson motorcycle are explored by Herbert Wagner in *At the Cre-*

ation: Myth, Reality, and the Origin of the Harley-Davidson Motorcycle, 1901–1909 (Madison: Wisconsin Historical Society Press, 2003).

Tourism is one of the main outcomes of these two innovations, as well as a major Wisconsin industry, and is thus extensively discussed in the literature. See J. H. H. Alexander, "Relax in Wisconsin, Friendly Land of Beauty," in *Wisconsin Blue Book, 1940*: 171–176; Isadore V. Fine and Edmund E. Werner, *The Tourist-Vacation Industry in Wisconsin*, Department of Resource Development (1961); Mary Lou Ballweg, "A Look at Wisconsin's Recreation Industry," in *Investor: Wisconsin's Business Magazine* 3 (June 1972): 32–36; and the dull-sounding but quite comprehensive and useful study by Ruth Goetz and Mary Kay Plantes, *Wisconsin Tourism Industry Study: [Part I] Background*, Department of Development (summary and six parts, 1983).

Commercial tourist accommodations are the subject of three studies by Lawrence G. Monthey in the *Transactions of the Wisconsin Academy of Sciences, Arts, and Letters*: "The Resort Industry of Wisconsin," in vol. 53, part A (1964): 79–99; "Trends in Wisconsin's Tourist-Lodging Industry," in vol. 58 (1970): 71–99; and, with Daniel Zielinski, "Vacation Resorts in Oneida County (Wisconsin): A Study of 1950–1968 Trends and Owner-operator Characteristics," in vol. 61 (1973): 207–227.

Tourist accounts of traveling through Wisconsin at various times are also useful for the glimpses at what attracted visitors and what kinds of accommodations awaited them. See, for instance, Increase Lapham, "An Early Journey through Sauk County," *Baraboo Daily News* (4 January 1912), and A. B. Braley, "Wisconsin Scenery," *Madison Democrat* (24 June 1879–6 July 1879). Old tourist booklets and travel books from the railways are also wonderful sources of information on tourism.

DEPRESSION

National surveys of the Great Depression and the various projects of the New Deal are numerous. One of the best, in part because of its relative shortness, is Eric Rauchway's *The Great Depression and the New Deal: A Very Short Introduction* (Oxford, UK, and New York: Oxford University Press, 2008). David M. Kennedy's *Freedom from Fear: The American People in Depression and War, 1929–1945* (New York: Oxford University Press, 2001) is an excellent synthesis of how the American people navigated two formative events, the Depression and the second World War. Two studies helpful in understanding the causes of the stock market collapse are John Kenneth Galbraith, *The Great Crash, 1929* (Boston: Houghton Mifflin, 1955; 50th anniversary ed. 1979), and Robert Sobel, *The Great Bull Market: Wall Street in the 1920s* (New York: Norton, 1968).

An introduction to how Wisconsin farmers responded to agricultural conditions in the 1930s is Walter H. Ebling's "Changes in Wisconsin Agriculture Since the Last Census," in *Wisconsin Blue Book, 1933*: 133–139. The milk strikes and violence that spread through rural areas of the state are described in Herbert Jacobs's "The Wisconsin Milk Strikes," *Wisconsin Magazine of History* 35 (Autumn 1951): 30–35. A. William Hoglund's "Wisconsin Dairy Farmers on Strike" in *Agricultural History* 35 (January 1961): 24–34, looks at the farmers' protest movement early in the Depression as well as the Wisconsin Cooperative Milk Pool.

For discussion of unemployment compensation law, see Daniel Nelson's "The Origins of Unemployment Insurance in Wisconsin," in *Wisconsin Magazine of History* 51 (Winter 1967–68): 109–121, and Nelson's later work, *Unemployment Insurance: The American Experience, 1915–1935* (Madison: University of Wisconsin Press, 1969).

The Wisconsin man celebrated as the "father of Social Security" is the subject of Theron F. Schlabach's *Edwin E. Witte: Cautious Reformer* (Madison: State Historical Society of Wisconsin, 1969). Arthur Altmeyer, who served on the Social Security Board and as commissioner of Social Security, linked the program with Wisconsin in "The Wisconsin Idea and Social Security," in *Wisconsin Magazine of History* 42 (Autumn 1958): 19–25. Altmeyer also wrote a book called *The Formative Years of Social Security* (Madison: University of Wisconsin Press, 1966).

The establishment of the Wisconsin Progressive Party during the Depression is discussed by Donald McCoy in "The Formation of the Wisconsin Progressive Party in 1934," *The Historian* 14 (Autumn 1951): 70–90, and J. C. Ralston, "Fierce Battle Waged over Name Choice," *Milwaukee Journal* (20 May 1934). For relationships between the Progressives and the New Dealers, see Otis L. Graham Jr., *An Encore for Reform: The Old Progressives and the New Deal* (New York: Oxford University Press, 1967).

And, of course, one of the best guides to Wisconsin in the 1930s is *The WPA Guide to Wisconsin* from the Federal Writers' Project of the Works Progress Administration (New York: Duell, Sloan, and Pearce, 1941; reprint Minnesota Historical Society Press, 2006).

WORLD WAR II

There are many good surveys of the national home front during the war, including: Richard Polenberg, *War and Society: The United States, 1941–1945* (Philadelphia: Lippincott, 1972); Geoffrey Perrett, *Days of Sadness, Years of Triumph: The American People, 1939–1945* (Madison: University of Wisconsin Press, 1985); and John Morton Blum, *V Was for Victory: Politics and American Culture During World War II* (New York: Harcourt Brace Jovanovich, 1976). Richard L. Pifer's *A City at War: Milwaukee Labor During WWII* (Madison: Wisconsin Historical Society Press, 2003) is an excellent city-specific study of the wartime effects.

Wartime letters and recollections are excellent sources of firsthand knowledge on home and battle front events. Three excellent volumes of wartime recollections are: *Voices of the Wisconsin Past: Women Remember the War, 1941–1945*, ed. Michael E. Stevens (Madison: Wisconsin Historical Society Press, 1993); *Voices of the Wisconsin Past: Remembering the Holocaust*, eds. Michael E. Stevens and Ellen Goldlust-Gingrich (Madison: Wisconsin Historical Society Press, 1997); and D. C. Everest Area Schools, *World War II: More Stories from Our Veterans* (Weston, WI: D. C. Everest Area Schools, 2004).

The Wisconsin Veterans Museum and the University of Wisconsin-Milwaukee have created an excellent online collection of previously unpublished letters available at www.uwm.edu/Library/arch/Warletters/wwII/WWII.htm. Richard Haney's *"When Is Daddy Coming Home?" An American Family During World War II* (Madison: Wisconsin Historical Society Press, 2005) explores the impact of the war on families through his own story of losing his father.

The authority on Manitowoc's submarines is William T. Nelson's *Fresh Water Submarines: The Manitowoc Story* (Manitowoc: Wisconsin Maritime Museum, 1986). See also Kathleen Warnes, "The Submarines of WWII," in *Inland Seas* 42 (Spring 1986): 12–23, and K. Jack Bauer, "Inland Seas and Overseas: Shipbuilding on the Great Lakes During World War II," in *Inland Seas*, 2 parts, 38 (Summer, Fall 1984): 84–94, 165–170.

For more on flying ace Richard Bong, see Carol Bong and Mike O'Conner, *Ace of Aces: The Dick Bong Story* (Mesa, AZ: Champlin Fighter Museum Press, 1985).

The most comprehensive look at Wisconsin's prisoner-of-war camps is Betty Cowley's *Stalag Wisconsin: Inside WWII Prisoner-of-war Camps* (Middleton, WI: Badger Books, 2002).

CULTURE OF FEAR

Few politicians have captured as much attention in the postwar period as Senator Joseph McCarthy. The best biographies of McCarthy are Thomas C. Reeves's *The Life and Times of Joe McCarthy: A Biography* (New York: Stein and Day, 1982), and David M. Oshinsky's *A Conspiracy So Immense: The World of Joe McCarthy* (New York: Free Press, 1983). Especially useful for Wisconsin is Michael O'Brien's *McCarthy and McCarthyism in Wisconsin* (Columbia: University of Missouri Press, 1980). Other helpful articles are Michael O'Brien, "Young Joe McCarthy, 1908–1944," *Wisconsin Magazine of History* 63 (Spring 1980): 179–232; Thomas C. Reeves, "The Search for Joe McCarthy," in *Wisconsin Magazine of History* 60 (Spring 1977): 185–196; and Reeves,

"Tail Gunner Joe: Joseph R. McCarthy and the Marine Corps," *Wisconsin Magazine of History* 62 (Summer 1979): 300–313. The opposition to and end of McCarthy is covered by David P. Thelan and Esther S. Thelan in "Joe Must Go: The Movement to Recall Senator Joseph R. McCarthy," *Wisconsin Magazine of History* 49 (Spring 1966): 185–209.

The Korean War, though not completely forgotten in the literature, has received far less attention than the two world wars. That said, Sarah A. Larsen and Jennifer M. Miller's *Wisconsin Korean War Stories: Veterans Tell Their Stories from the Forgotten War* (Madison: Wisconsin Historical Society Press, 2008), and D. C. Everest Area Schools' *Korean War Not Forgotten: Stories from Korean War Veterans* (Weston, WI: D. C. Everest Area School District Oral History Project, 2003) are unmatched sources of firsthand experiences.

The Wisconsin Historical Museum's online exhibit "Living Under a Mushroom Cloud: Fear and Hope in the Atomic Age," at www .wisconsinhistory.org/museum/atomic/ explores the fears and hopes that gripped the nation during the Cold War.

MIGRATION AND CIVIL RIGHTS

There aren't yet any comprehensive histories of blacks in Wisconsin, though there are a number of good works on particular black communities. Joe William Trotter Jr.'s *Black Milwaukee: The Making of an Industrial Proletariat, 1915–45* (Urbana and Chicago: University of Illinois Press, 1985) is a thorough account whether or not you accept the argument of his subtitle. Another book about black Milwaukee is Frank Aukofer's *City with a Chance* (Milwaukee: Marquette University Press, 1968; 2nd ed. 2007), a popularly written account of the civil rights movement. Thomas C. McCormick and Richard A. Hornseth's "The Negro in Madison, Wisconsin," *American Sociological Review* 12 (October 1947): 519–525, is the best source for the early history of blacks in Madison. Zachary Cooper's *Black Settlers in Rural Wisconsin* (Madison: State Historical Society of Wisconsin, 1977) is the first to deal with rural black settlements in Wisconsin.

A starting place for statistical information on blacks is Mary Lou Kendrigan's *The Negro in Wisconsin: A Statistical Profile*, Library Reference Bureau, Wisconsin Briefs, no. 66–2 (1966).

Primary research on African Americans is relatively sparse prior to 1960; records and published reports of the Fair Employment Practices Division of the Wisconsin Industrial Commission and the Governor's Commission on Human Rights, both state agencies, are the most helpful.

Valuable sources for black viewpoints are a series of in-depth stories in the Milwaukee newspapers. See, for example, "The Negro Speaks," a six-part series published between December 10 and 15, 1962, in the *Milwaukee Sentinel*, and "As Milwaukee Negroes See It," an eight-part series published between February 6 and 13, 1966, in the *Milwaukee Journal*. The experiences of African Americans in Madison, particularly after their forced relocation from the Greenbush neighborhood for urban renewal projects, is covered in two series of newspaper articles: "The Negro in Madison," *Wisconsin State Journal* (July 28–August 25, 1963) and "Madison Blacks," *Wisconsin State Journal* (July 10–17, 1983). The twenty-year span between the two series provides an interesting perspective on the situation and its aftermath.

Concerning the race riots in Milwaukee, see Karl H. Flaming, *Who "Riots" and Why? Black and White Perspectives in Milwaukee* (Milwaukee: Milwaukee Urban League, 1968); Jonathan A. Slesinger, *Study of Community Opinions Concerning the Summer 1967 Civil Disturbance in Milwaukee* (Milwaukee: University of Wisconsin-Milwaukee, 1968); and Aukofer's previously mentioned *City with a Chance*.

Efforts to resolve the confrontations over housing are discussed by Jeffrey B. Bartell, Charles A. Buss, and Edward R. Stege Jr., "The Mediation of Civil Rights Disputes: Open Housing in Milwaukee," *Wisconsin Law Review 1968* (Fall 1968): 1127–1191. Richard Bernard and Bill Lueders describe the marches and earlier confrontations in "The Selma of the North," *Milwaukee Magazine* 11 (February 1986): 74–80.

VIETNAM

The story of Wisconsin in Vietnam has yet to be written, but David Maraniss's *They Marched into Sunlight: War and Peace, Vietnam and America, October 1967* (New York: Simon & Schuster, 2003) provides a powerful counterpoint of battlefront and home front events in Vietnam, Washington, D.C., and Madison. The documentary *The War At Home* (Catalyst Films/Madison Film, 1979) uses archival footage and interviews with public figures to show what happened in Madison in the 1960s and early 1970s as students and community members began to protest the war.

Letters and recollections are rich sources of information on wartime experiences. The stories of ninety-two Wisconsin men and women are told in *Voices from Vietnam*, ed. Michael Stevens (Madison: Wisconsin Historical Society Press, 1996). Dale Reich recalls his time in Vietnam in "One Year in Vietnam: A Young Soldier Remembers," *Wisconsin Magazine of History* 64 (Spring 1981): 161–179, and in his later book *Rockets like Rain: A Year in Vietnam* (Ashland, OR: Hellgate Press, 2001). The Wisconsin Veterans Museum and the University of Wisconsin-Milwaukee produced an online collection entitled "Wisconsin War Letters: Vietnam" of previously unpublished letters from Wisconsin soldiers and their families, online at http://www.uwm.edu/Library/arch/Warletters/vietnam/Vietnam.htm.

Newspaper reports in the *Wisconsin State Journal* and the *Capital Times* are the best source for accounts of the Sterling Hall bombing. The bombing is recalled in "Revisiting Sterling Hall," *Wisconsin Magazine of History* 90 (Autumn 2006): 52–53, an article describing an exhibit on the bombing. The 1998 documentary *The Bombing of Sterling Hall* (Leemark Communication) explores the climate on campus before and after the bombing and interviews many of the people involved.

*   *   *

GREENING WISCONSIN

One of the best odes to the Wisconsin environment comes from William Cronon in "Landscape and Home: Environmental Traditions in Wisconsin," *Wisconsin Magazine of History* 74 (Winter 1990–91): 82–105. Personal attachment to the land is also the subject of William David Barillas's *The Midwestern Pastoral: Place and Landscape in Literature of the American Heartland* (Athens: Ohio University Press, 2006).

Key figures in Wisconsin's environmental movement are the subject of numerous books and articles, in addition to the often prodigious number of writings they produced themselves.

Wisconsin's first environmentalist, Increase Lapham, is profiled by Milo M. Quaife in "Increase Allen Lapham, First Scholar of Wisconsin," *Wisconsin Magazine of History* 1 (September 1917): 3–15, and by Erika Janik in "Citizen Scientist," *Wisconsin Natural Resources Magazine* (February 2007). Lapham's own works on environmental issues include: "The Forest Trees of Wisconsin" in *Transactions of the Wisconsin State Agricultural Society* 4 (Madison: Wisconsin State Agricultural Society, 1858): 195–251; and *Report on the Disastrous Effects of the Destruction of Forest Trees, now Going on so Rapidly in the State of Wisconsin* (Madison: Atwood & Rublee, 1867).

Aldo Leopold's seminal work, *A Sand County Almanac: And Sketches Here and There* (New York: Oxford University Press, 1949), is an essential study of the land around Sauk County as well as his environmental theory. Leopold's biographers include: Julianne Lutz Newton, *Aldo Leopold's Odyssey* (Washington, D.C.: Island Press, 2006); Marybeth Lorbiecki, *Aldo Leopold: A Fierce Green Fire* (Guilford, CT: Globe Pequot, 2004); Susan L. Flader, *Thinking Like a Mountain: Aldo Leopold and the Evolution of an Ecological Attitude Toward Deer, Wolves, and Forests* (Columbia: University of Missouri Press, 1974); and Susan Flader, "The Person and the Place," in Anthony Wolff, ed., *The Sand Country of Aldo Leopold: A Photographic Interpre-*

tation by Charles Steinhacker (San Francisco: Sierra Club, 1973). Besides the *Sand County Almanac, The Essential Aldo Leopold: Quotations and Commentaries*, eds., Curt Meine and Richard L. Knight (Madison: University of Wisconsin Press, 1999) provides a broad portrait of Leopold's philosophy.

The best biography of John Muir is Donald Worster's *A Passion for Nature: The Life of John Muir* (Oxford, UK, and New York: Oxford University Press, 2008). Muir's own memoir, *The Story of My Boyhood and Youth* (Boston & New York: Houghton Mifflin Company, 1913), describes how his childhood in Wisconsin helped to spark his scientific curiosity and reverence for nature.

Bill Christofferson's *The Man from Clear Lake: Earth Day Founder Senator Gaylord Nelson* (Madison: University of Wisconsin Press, 2004) is a good starting place for learning about the man behind Earth Day. See also Nelson's own *Beyond Earth Day: Fulfilling the Promise* (Madison: University of Wisconsin Press, 2002) and *America's Last Chance* (Waukesha, WI: Country Beautiful Corp, 1970). In 1980, Nelson wrote a short retrospective on the first Earth Day, "Earth Day '70: What It Meant," *EPA Journal* (April 1980).

THE CHANGING FACE OF IMMIGRATION

Of the literally hundreds of published works on Wisconsin's ethnic history, few go beyond the early twentieth century; the ones that do are often written in fields other than history.

On Poles in Wisconsin, see Samuel Bonikowski's "The Polish Press in Wisconsin," in *Polish American Studies* 2 (January–June 1945): 12–23; Richard Zeitlin, "White Eagles in the North Woods: Polish Immigration to Rural Wisconsin, 1857–1900," in *Polish Review* 25 (no. 1, 1980): 69–92; Frank Hayden Miller, "The Polanders in Wisconsin," *Parkman Club no. 10* (Milwaukee: Parkman Club, 1896); Donald Pienkos, "Politics, Religion and Change in Polish Milwaukee," *Wisconsin Magazine of History* 61 (Spring 1978): 178–209; and Donald Pienkos, "Dimensions of Ethnicity: Preliminary Report on the Milwaukee Polish American Population," in *Polish American Studies* 30 (Spring 1973): 5–19.

The literature on Wisconsin's Hispanic community remains woefully sparse despite the fact that this population is the state's fastest growing. The best place to start is Cristobal S. Berry-Caban's *Hispanics in Wisconsin: A Bibliography of Resource Materials* (Madison: Wisconsin Historical Society Press, 1981), which lists all items about, for, or by Hispanics in Wisconsin. On migrant labor, see Doris P. Slesinger and Eileen Muirragui's *Migrant Agricultural Labor in Wisconsin: A Short History* (Madison: University of Wisconsin-Madison Institute for Research on Poverty, 1979). In 1929, social worker Agnes Fenton visited Mexican families living in Milwaukee and published a report on her observations and findings: *The Mexicans of the City of Milwaukee, Wisconsin* (Milwaukee: YWCA International Institute, 1930). For perspective, see John Gurda's study done fifty years later: "The Latin Community on Milwaukee's Near South Side," Milwaukee Urban Observatory (Milwaukee: University of Milwaukee, 1976).

Smaller ethnic groups have not been completely neglected. On Italians, see "Biggest Farm Italian Colony in this State," *Milwaukee-Wisconsin News* (27 January 1924) and "Village of Genoa Picturesque Town in which First Settlers were Natives of Italian Alps," *La Crosse Tribune and Leader-Press* (20 July 1930). On Czechs, see Karel D. Bicha, "The Czechs in Wisconsin History," in *Wisconsin Magazine of History* 53 (Spring 1970): 194–203. On Greeks in Milwaukee, see Theodore Saloutos, "The Greeks of Milwaukee," *Wisconsin Magazine of History* 53 (Spring 1970): 175–193.

The Hmong experience is vividly recalled in *The Hmong and Their Stories: The Secret Wars, Escape to Laos, the Legends*, by the D. C. Everest Hmong Oral History Project (Weston, WI: D. C. Everest Area Schools, 2001). For an overview on Hmong history and transition to America, see Tim Pfaff's *Hmong in America* (Eau Claire, WI: Chippewa Valley Museum Press, 2005). Hmong refugees in La Crosse are the subject of Denis Lee Tucker's *The History and Status of Indochinese Refugees in La Crosse, Wisconsin* (La Crosse: La Crosse Area

Hmong Mutual Assistance Association), which details Hmong history, reviews some of the principal difficulties faced by refugees, and discusses services available to them in the community.

INDIAN TREATY RIGHTS

Nancy Oestreich Lurie details Wisconsin Indian affairs, from the founding of the United States through the beginning of the twenty-first century, in her seminal work, *Wisconsin Indians: Revised and Expanded Edition* (Madison: Wisconsin Historical Society Press, 2002). Patty Loew's *Indian Nations of Wisconsin: Histories of Endurance and Renewal* (Madison: Wisconsin Historical Society Press, 2001) follows each of the state's tribes from origin stories to contemporary struggles over treaty rights and sovereignty issues. See also William H. Hodge's "The Indians of Wisconsin," *Wisconsin Blue Book, 1975*: 95–196. Other useful books focus on a single tribe, including Edmund J. Danziger Jr., *The Chippewas of Lake Superior* (Norman: University of Oklahoma Press, 1978), and Patricia K. Ourada, *The Menominee Indians: A History* (Norman: University of Oklahoma Press, 1979).

The best single work on treaty rights in Wisconsin, tracing U.S. and Ojibwe relations from the early nineteenth century to 1991, is Ronald N. Satz's "Chippewa Treaty Rights: The Reserved Rights of Wisconsin's Chippewa Indians in Historical Perspective," *Transactions of the Wisconsin Academy of Sciences, Arts and Letters* 29 (Madison: Wisconsin Academy of Sciences, Arts and Letters, 1991): 1–251. *Moving Beyond Argument: Racism and Treaty Rights* (Odanah, WI: Great Lakes Indian Fish & Wildlife Commission, 1989) is a series of articles about some of the major treaty issues. A series of articles in the *Wisconsin State Journal*, "Treaty Crisis: Cultures in Conflict" (1990), examined the people, places, and politics of the treaty issue.

For more on the Menominee and termination, see "Bill Is Seen as Threat to Indian Lands," *Milwaukee Journal* (22 February 1925); Clifford F. Butcher, "Now the Menominee Indians Are Ready to Govern Themselves," *Milwaukee Journal* (16 June 1935); and Melvin L.

Robertson, *A Brief Story of the Menominee Indians* (Keshena, WI: Menominee Indian Agency, 1958).

POSTWAR POLITICS AND THE CONSERVATIVE REVOLUTION

Newspapers and the papers of elected officials are often the best place to go for basic primary research on state politics and political thought. The best source for election totals is the *Wisconsin Blue Books*, which also contain brief biographies of elected officials.

Leon D. Epstein's *Politics in Wisconsin* (Madison: University of Wisconsin Press, 1958) was written before it became clear that Wisconsin was on its way to becoming a two-party state but remains an important source. As is Epstein's "A Two-Party Wisconsin?" in *The Journal of Politics* 18 (August 1956): 427–458; Richard C. Haney, "The Rise of Wisconsin's New Democrats: A Political Realignment in the Mid-Twentieth Century," *Wisconsin Magazine of History* 58 (Winter 1974–75): 90–106; and David L. Brye, *Wisconsin Voting Patterns in the Twentieth Century, 1900 to 1950* (New York: Garland, 1979).

INDEX

ERIKA JANIK is the author of *Odd Wisconsin: Amusing, Perplexing and Unlikely Stories from Wisconsin's Past*, published by the Wisconsin Historical Society Press. Her work has appeared in *Midwest Living, MyMidwest, Wisconsin Trails*, the *Wisconsin State Journal, Wisconsin Magazine of History*, and *The Onion*. Originally from Redmond, Washington, she now lives in Madison.